www.wadsworth.com

www.wadsworth.com is the World Wide Web site for Thomson Wadsworth and is your direct source to dozens of online resources.

At *www.wadsworth.com* you can find out about supplements, demonstration software, and student resources. You can also send email to many of our authors and preview new publications and exciting new technologies.

www.wadsworth.com
Changing the way the world learns®

Current Perspectives
Readings from InfoTrac® College Edition

Crisis Management and National Emergency Response

SABINA L. BURTON
University of California, Irvine

THOMSON ™

WADSWORTH

Australia • Brazil • Canada • Mexico • Singapore • Spain
United Kingdom • United States

THOMSON
™
WADSWORTH

Current Perspectives: Readings from InfoTrac®
College Edition: Crisis Management and National Emergency Response
Sabina L. Burton

Senior Acquisitions Editor: *Carolyn Henderson Meier*
Assistant Editor: *Jana Davis*
Editorial Assistant: *Rebecca Johnson*
Technology Project Manager: *Susan DeVanna*
Marketing Manager: *Terra Schultz*
Marketing Assistant: *Jaren Boland*
Marketing Communications Manager: *Linda Yip*
Project Manager, Editorial Production: *Iris Sandilands*

Creative Director: *Rob Hugel*
Print Buyer: *Linda Hsu*
Permissions Editor: *Joohee Lee*
Production Service: *Ruchika Vij, Interactive Composition Corporation*
Cover Designer: *Larry Didona*
Cover Image: *Photolibrary.com/Photonica*
Cover and Text Printer: *Thomson West*
Compositor: *Interactive Composition Corporation*

Printed in the United States of America
1 2 3 4 5 6 7 10 09 08 07 06

Library of Congress Control Number: 2005937226

ISBN 0-495-12996-8

Thomson Higher Education
10 Davis Drive
Belmont, CA 94002-3098
USA

For more information about our products, contact us at:
Thomson Learning Academic Resource Center
1-800-423-0563

For permission to use material from this text or product, submit a request online at
http://www.thomsonrights.com.

Any additional questions about permissions can be submitted by e-mail to
thomsonrights@thomson.com.

Contents

IV. DEALING WITH THE TRAUMA   45

V. DISASTER RESPONSE: CRITICISM AND RECOMMENDATIONS   65

Preface

CRISIS MANAGEMENT AND NATIONAL DISASTER RESPONSE

Our national and state crisis response teams have been sorely tested the last few years. Floodings in the Midwest and gulf region have destroyed many lives, homes and businesses, earthquakes in California have caused injuries and structural damage and severe winter storms on the East Coast have shut down operations for weeks. Police, Crash/Fire and Rescue units, Federal Emergency Management Agency (FEMA) and Firefighters have been tested by the terrorist attacks on September 11, 2001, the Oklahoma City bombing, natural disasters, factory explosions, hazardous waste spills and various other isolated disasters; sometimes failing the test. With the looming specters of terrorism, elevated risk of damage due to earthquakes and global warming spawned destructive weather patterns crisis management may be the most important civil issue we must address in the 21st century.

Crisis management is a relatively new field of management. Its proactive measures include identifying weaknesses in the system and preparing for potential disasters to reduce the vulnerability of our infrastructure to natural catastrophes or terroristic attacks. Its reactive measures include deployment of personnel and execution of scenario driven planning. Failure to plan equates to failure to execute. Failure of crisis management is devastating to search and rescue attempts and allows damage that otherwise could have been averted. Areas of potential failure are many; the loss of communications and computer systems and damage to transportation systems are just a few of the most obvious. Beyond the technical and structural aspects crisis response includes counseling for the traumatized, re-establishment of law and order and public relations to restore trust in the government.

When disasters occur local and state departments work alongside FEMA to respond quickly and efficiently. A new networking technology created in the early 1990s has improved the processing of information and allocation of resources. When necessary, FEMA will recommend that the president make a disaster declaration to authorize mobilization of additional assets. The National Guard and other branches of the military can be mobilized to help local authorities to respond to the needs in the affected region. In spite of these advances in crisis preparedness the devastating attacks on the World Trade Center in New York by al Qaeda terrorists on September 11, 2001 and the recent destruction caused by hurricane Katrina in the gulf region in August of 2005 clearly overwhelmed the system. We no longer feel prepared and ready. More and more voices demand that we plan for the unthinkable, that we be ready mentally and physically.

This reader was put together to enable the student of this field to draw information from many different sources. The articles chosen from InfoTrac by Thomson discuss various aspects of crisis management: problems arising from disasters, identification and apprehension of predators who are trying to take advantage of a downed system, riot-control, the emotional and physical exhaustion of police and rescue workers, and critical assessment of our disaster response programs. Most of the articles were published fairly recently. A few older publications were carefully selected to address the multiple facades of crises.

The first part of the reader is called **The Disasters after the Disaster**:

Dealing with trauma is not the only burden that police officers face when responding to catastrophes. Communication is an essential tool in organizing search and rescue operations as well as coordinating law enforcement efforts. Responding to natural disasters, terroristic attacks, enormous fires and riots challenge the logistics of any agency. *"Duty Binds Officers Who Have Gone to Help After Storm"* report about the problem of meeting the many needs and the creativity of the people in uniform who rise to the challenge. Failing radios and phone services add to the hardship of coordinating the numerous officers and volunteers, many of whom have traveled great distances to offer their services and support. The articles *"MIS managers help in earthquake-rocked city"* points out similar problems after the 1989 San Francisco earthquake. The desperate measures taken to handle the masses of dislocated people are the subject of the article *"Police in Suburbs Blocked Evacuees, Witnesses Report."* Relocating several hundreds of thousands of citizens and providing them with food and temporary shelter creates a seemingly unmanageable task for the police. Evacuations never go exactly as planned either. Upset and confused citizens, wary of leaving their homes are often ready to defend their decision to stay by force. With the chaos comes the lawlessness and the police must respond with deadly force as described in the next four articles *"Police Begin Seizing Guns Of Civilians," "New Orleans Police Kill 4 in Shootout," "DJ New Orleans Sending In More Police To Stem Tide Of Looting"* and *"Midwest Police Face Trouble with Traffic, Not Looting."*

The next two articles address the problem of cashing in on disasters and appear under the heading of **Dealing with Scam-Artists**. In *"Hurricane Fraud Cases Surprise Even Officials"* and *"After the Storm, the Swindlers"* the authors introduce the many ways con artists took advantage of Federal and

State programs designed to assist people in need after the recent hurricane disasters and prey on the empathy of others who willingly donated to fake charities for Hurricane Katrina victims.

Responding to Riots discusses another form of crisis that is a major challenge to law enforcement and that in many ways mirrors the distraction and trauma associated with natural disasters and catastrophes. The article "*In L.A., Trying to Keep a Lid on Racial Strife*" outlines the dilemma many police agencies face of being haunted by past mistakes and acts of brutality on the one hand and misconceptions in the communities. Though most law enforcement departments today subscribe to some form of community policing there is still much to do to bridge the gap between the police and our less affluent mainly minority neighborhoods. As we know from the recent disasters those racially diverse neighborhoods tend to bear the brunt of destruction and chaos. Tensions between the police and minority communities hampering the efforts of maintaining law and order after national disasters strike. The line between crime control and observation of individual rights is fine and difficult to walk. Similar observations are shared by the article "*More Risk Management Urged for L.A. Cops.*" The needs of rescue workers and community members must be properly assessed and combined with a community sensitive approach in our response to rioting. In "*Boston Faces Riot-Control Test,*" the author describes the destructive power of the mob. So called "hooliganistic" crowds, a rather European phenomenon, test law enforcement's ability to properly and effectively police the masses. In response to extreme drinking on campuses, the author asks also who should be responsible for preventive mob control measures, team owners, athletes, the city, or the police? The article "*Police to Use Containment Pens to Handle Protest*" describes a questionable practice of crowd control that clearly indicates the need for better management of such incidents.

The next set of articles are combined under the header of **Dealing with the Trauma**. Crisis management must also include a sophisticated support system for those who provide services to the battered community. The articles include among others the accounts of New Orleans police officers who have worked feverishly around the clock to help rescue people in need and restore some sense of order. There was no time to think of your own needs or pains. When these brave men and women finally got a break the realization of their own losses of loved ones, homes, and possessions hit even harder. These strains added to the destabilizing forces of destruction, overwhelming demands, and understaffing that left the police department of New Orleans crippled as "*Scarred Police Force Tries to Regroup after Storm*" reports. "*With Some Now at Breaking Point, City's Officers Tell of Pain and Pressure*" and "*Police Quitting, Overwhelmed by Chaos*" deal with the enormous stress of responding to destruction, human death and suffering day after day. The mental and physical exhaustion combined with the feeling of helplessness and sorrow became so overwhelming to some of them that they had to walk away from their job, or even worse, could not go on with their lives anymore. "*The Grief Police*" and "*PTSD rate Tripled Among N.Y. Police Officers*" describes a similar picture for officers who responded to the World Trade Center attacks in 2001. Recognizing the need for support officials must watch out, however, to not further burden the responding police personnel with "overzealous mental-health professionals" who may do more harm than good.

The last part of the Crisis Management Reader deals with articles to **Disaster Response: Criticism and Recommendations**. The article "*Mayor's Plan Puts Police Commissioner in Charge of Disaster Control*" describes efforts to coordinate multi-agency responses under one leadership to improve the handling of crisis situations. These efforts were based on two 9/11 reports discussed in "*9/11 Exposes Deadly Flaws in Rescue Plan*" and "*Report on 9/11 finds flaws in response of Police Department.*" The articles point out shortcomings in logistics, training, and maintenance. The NYPD also lacked training in responding to large scale disasters and lacks leadership and guidance in handling such a difficult challenge. "*Expanding Federal Power: The Real Lessons of Hurricane Katrina*" and "*Improving Emergency Responsiveness with Management Science*" are detailed assessment of current emergency responses and provides recommendations for improvement.

It is the hope of the publisher to assist researchers of this subject in their studies and make readers aware of the urgency of crisis management.

I

THE DISASTERS AFTER THE DISASTER

When a disaster strikes, the hurricane, earthquake, or terrorist attack is often just the beginning of the damage. A quick response could minimize damage whereas poor planning and inappropriate execution could create an environment that exacerbates the destruction. Police and rescue personnel are faced with the immense task of rescuing the injured; recovering the dead; providing food, shelter, counseling, and security to the displaced; and confronting those individuals who prey on the weak. Chaos and lawlessness all too often follow catastrophes. The police struggle to meet the demands of calming the masses, dispersing hysteria, and enforcing the law while dealing with severe breakdowns of the infrastructure and many other physical and psychological challenges.

1

Duty Binds Officers Who Have Gone to Help After Storm

Al Baker

On Toulouse and North Rampart Streets in the French Quarter, a Michigan police car nosed behind a New York City Police Department truck parked outside the New Orleans Police Department's First District.

"They're coming from Michigan and New York and everywhere," Aaron Wiltz, a patrolman with the New Orleans Police Department, said as he surveyed the scene. "It's just awesome. Just to see them sitting next to each other; if I had a word for it, I'd tell you, but it's just nice to see."

Almost two weeks after the devastation brought by Hurricane Katrina, a hodgepodge army of law enforcement officers from around the country have converged on this city to help its besieged police force restore order. About 10,000 local, state and federal officers—from close-in locations in like Louisiana, Mississippi, Alabama and Arkansas and Georgia, and as far away as Illinois, New Mexico and California—are patrolling the streets and helping the search-and-rescue efforts.

"The men and women who are here know their jobs and do it very well," said Capt. Marlon A. Defillo, a spokesman for the New Orleans Police Department. "A robbery in New Orleans is the same as a robbery in Los Angeles. All you are doing is changing the name of the locale."

For days after Hurricane Katrina blew in and tore the city apart, communications for Officer Wiltz and his colleagues came undone. Cellular antennas bent like bows or fell, causing cellphones to sputter and go silent; and the roots of upended trees tore out underground wires, essentially reducing police radios to hunks of plastic.

Some in the city exploited the breakdowns by forming gangs that spread violence. New Orleans experienced a crime wave, with reports of looting, rapes, assaults and the theft of entire inventories from gun and ammunition shops.

The New Orleans police force can normally muster 1,500 officers. But scores of them were off duty or cut off by the storm and flood waters. Police officials also said that a number of officers resigned or simply walked off their posts in the days after the storm. Last weekend, two officers committed suicide.

Offers of help from other law enforcement agencies came within hours of the storm, but it took days in some cases for the waters to recede enough to allow the reinforcements to reach the city.

Visiting officers set up makeshift camps and emergency operations centers in the parishes around New Orleans and beyond.

The 303-member contingent from New York City, which includes an assistant chief of police and three inspectors, have based their operations in an abandoned nursing home in Harahan, La., about 10 miles west of New Orleans.

On Wednesday, 25 vanloads of New York officers drove from Harahan into New Orleans and took up patrolling the French Quarter.

They joined a law enforcement effort that not only includes the New Orleans police, officers from other in-state jurisdictions like Baton Rouge and thousands of out-of-state officers, but also members of the National Guard.

The Guard has had an increasingly heavy presence in the city, said Captain Defillo, the spokesman for the New Orleans Police Department. At night, the troops walk in small groups in the Garden District or the French Quarter, dressed in camouflage, carrying weapons, or driving Humvees, giving the feel of a militarized zone.

Sgt. Mark G. Mix, a spokesman for the Louisiana State Police, said that about 4,000 troops from Louisiana and Arkansas were doing search and rescue and "a lot of police work."

There is a natural camaraderie between the officers. "That also holds true for the military," New York City's police commissioner, Raymond W. Kelly, said in a telephone interview on Thursday.

When their beats cross, police officers and soldiers usually communicate with a wave, a smile or a quick greeting, as when a police cruiser passes a military checkpoint and the officers say: "Stay safe," or "Good evening, gents."

But bringing separate police agencies into a single city under a unified command is not without its difficulties, several officials said. Early on, the task was like trying to join bits of naturally repelling mercury.

The officers' radio frequencies were incompatible. Their jargon was different, their cultures apart and the landscape foreign.

Ron Hernandez, a New York officer who usually works in Manhattan, said he had been taken aback when he arrived in Harahan to see so many civilians with guns casually strapped to their hips.

But slowly, small groups of officers linked up and traded information. Sheriffs joined with sheriffs. State police officers gravitated toward one another and fire department officials joined other fire officials, Sergeant Mix of the Louisiana State Police said.

To help coordinate, Officer Jim Byrne, of the New York police communications division, brought hundreds of the department's radios to Louisiana. Within hours of arriving, he and his crew had linked an antenna to a mast on their temporary headquarters, a Winnebago-like truck, and mounted another antenna on a building in nearby Westwego to expand the coverage area. Phone lines from a vacant pizzeria were commandeered. A Harahan police radio was placed inside the truck to get dispatches from the local officers.

The patchwork of agencies is being held together by New Orleans police commanders at Harrah's Casino, which has been turned into a temporary command post. The casino houses the top officials from several agencies who meet each morning to deploy people.

"All the key individuals are in the room," said Captain Defillo, including Michael Holt, the special agent in charge of immigration, customs and enforcement for the federal Department of Homeland Security. "The left hand knows what the right hand knows."

It is difficult to say how long each of the agencies will remain here, or whether others will arrive.

Police officials in New Orleans said the law enforcement agencies would have to make individual decisions about how long to stay and whether to rotate their officers in and out. But Captain Defillo said it appeared the agencies were here for an indefinite stay.

"We have got no word on them leaving, none," he said. "Everyone we have spoken with is prepared for the long haul."

2

MIS Managers Help
in Earthquake-Rocked City

Mary E. Thyfault

Abstract: *MIS managers were the unsung heros of the Oct 17, 1989, San Francisco earthquake. They stabilized many of the city's crucial computer systems following the 7.0 jolt that knocked out most of the utilities in the Bay Area. The first priority for MIS was finding alternative power sources to keep systems going. The police department's back-up generator kept its IBM 4381-based call-management system working. The Federal Reserve had already saved the day's transactions following a shift change, and its Fedwire was working normally the following day. The FAA maintained its technical computers through its IBM host computer across the bay.*

S AN FRANCISCO—The Bay area's heroes were no longer the Giants or Athletics, but the fire-fighters, police, hospital workers, and other resources who brought San Francisco out of the rubble of the country's second-worst earthquake last week. MIS managers became the invisible heroes here, trying to stabilize the city's most critical computer systems, in an era when operations have grown so dependent on high technology.

And MIS managers fought to make those systems operate, providing the tools to pull San Francisco out of the crisis. Seeking alternate power sources to keep computer systems running became the first priority.

"If you don't have power, you don't have the ability to manage your information," said Capt. Walter Cullop, commander of the Technical Services Division of the San Francisco Police Department. "During a crisis, we are the eyes and the ears of the city."

MIS Week, Oct 23, 1989 v10 n42 p1(2) "MIS Managers Help in Earthquake-Rocked City" by Mary E. Thyfault. © Fairchild Publications Inc. 1989.

The police's back-up generator—always on hand, Cullop said—kept the department's all-important IBM 4381-based call-management system up and running. "We never missed a beat," he said. However, dispatchers did have to "go to little slips of paper off and on" to route the calls when Cullop brought the system down six times over a two-day-period to switch power supplies.

THE SHOW GOES ON

The *San Francisco Chronicle* and *San Francisco Examiner*, the city's morning and evening newspapers respectively, scrambled to find generators and an alternative to their jointly-owned 11-year-old Systems Integrators Inc. (SII) System 55 publishing system. The newspaper's staff mixed low- and high-technology using flashlights, generators, Tandy laptops, Macintosh IIs and a satellite to create a paper that was printed 30 miles away for the information hungry city.

"The Chronicle of October 18, 1989, is a newspaper produced with a heavy heart," said Executive Editor William German on the front page of the day's 16-page Extra edition. "The fact that it was produced at all was a mighty feat. This awful blow wiped out the tools of modern journalism. No magic computers, no push-button presses, not even lights to see by."

The San Francisco office of the Federal Reserve had timing on its side. The Fed not only had a back-up generator, but because the quake happened during a shift change, all of the employees had just stored the data on which they had been working. "Most of our computers are on an 'auto save' anyway," said a spokesman. A spokeswoman said the Fedwire, the central bank's funds and securities transfer service, was operating normally nationwide the following day. It was "business as usual Wednesday," the spokesman said.

The Pacific Stock Exchange traded only "those issues focused on in San Francisco" after suffering structural damages in the quake, according to a spokesman. Its equity trading operations were rerouted to Los Angeles. The exchange said it would attempt to transfer options trading to other exchanges on a temporary basis.

San Francisco foreign exchange customers were rerouted to the Los Angeles trading room. While a spokesman said that they hoped to return to normal as soon as possible, he could not elaborate by press time on whether the internal systems were damaged.

The Bank of America said that while its world headquarters was closed Wednesday, customers could access automated-teller machines throughout the state, except in areas where the power was out.

FAA FLIES WITH IBM

The Federal Aviation Administration control tower had no problems accessing its IBM host computer in Fremont, Ca. "We didn't have any outages in technical computers," said Ed Lewis, San Francisco Air Traffic Manager.

However, the control tower did lose less vital computers—an IBM PC that monitors the technical system and an administrative Comet PC. "They've been trashed . . . they both fell off the table and broke." A new IBM PC arrived Friday and Lewis is trying to get the Comet fixed. The FAA had a back-up generator that kicked in as soon as power went down

Comdisco Disaster Recovery Services of Rosemont, Ill., said that three banks, two manufacturing firms and two distribution firms have been declared disasters. The company is expecting seven more companies to declare disasters.

After the earthquake struck, the city turned off its power supply until the Pacific Gas and Electric Company (PG&E) could inspect buildings for gas leaks. When the city power supply goes down, all of Pacific Bell's switches automatically go to battery for several hours. However, once the battery goes down, a person must manually start a generator at the switching center.

As a result, a central office (CO) in Holister, near the epicenter of the quake, was down for seven hours and a San Francisco CO was down for a "short time," according to Pacific Bell spokesperson Dianna Wentworth.

"The net is up and working," she said at eleven o'clock Tuesday morning. "For the most part, the problems have been the sheer volume of calls," causing switches on the network to either automatically or manually block calls to "load control" the lines. As a result, customers may get "fast busy signals," indicating that the circuits are busy. Many customers also had to wait two to three seconds for dial tones to become free.

LONG DISTANCE CARRIERS ALSO REPORTED DELAYS BECAUSE OF THE PAC BELL DELAYS

US Sprint reported that while their network was fully operational, Pac Bell was blocking customer calls. Some Telenet customers were also not receiving the service because of power outages. However, telephone service was only one of the problems that the *Chronicle*, which could only use about 30 of its 200 phones, had to overcome to perform its daily function, which grew even more critical in the crisis.

"The public wants to know," said Managing Editor Matt Wilson. "We managed to print 600,000 copies . . . of good, solid, useful, meaningful information for people whose lives have been threatened."

The newspaper staff managed to beat the run on batteries and flashlights at the nearby hardware store, saving the paper from returning to the dark ages.

The next priority was finding generators. The paper used "two-to-four generators," Williams said, adding he was not sure where they all came from.

As reporters phoned in information, writers used 12 Tandy portable laptops to create the stories. Then one-by-one, the stories were communicated to the Art Department's network of five Macintosh IIs. Headlines and picture captions were also written on the Macs.

Copy was printed out on a Laserwriter. The Art department then redis-covered the ruler as they placed the copy on the pages by hand, instead of the computerized system. The pages were photographed and then sent via satel-lite by a Page Fax to the printing plant 30 miles away.

"At one point, we weren't sure the satellite was going to work and we were talking about getting a boat to get stuff to the East Bay," said City Editor Daniel Rosenheim.

3

Police in Suburbs Blocked Evacuees, Witnesses Report

Gardiner Harris

Police agencies to the south of New Orleans were so fearful of the crowds trying to leave the city after Hurricane Katrina that they sealed a crucial bridge over the Mississippi River and turned back hundreds of desperate evacuees, two paramedics who were in the crowd said.

The paramedics and two other witnesses said officers sometimes shot guns over the heads of fleeing people, who, instead of complying immediately with orders to leave the bridge, pleaded to be let through, the paramedics and two other witnesses said. The witnesses said they had been told by the New Orleans police to cross that same bridge because buses were waiting for them there.

Instead, a suburban police officer angrily ordered about 200 people to abandon an encampment between the highways near the bridge. The officer then confiscated their food and water, the four witnesses said. The incidents took place in the first days after the storm last week, they said.

"The police kept saying, 'We don't want another Superdome,' and 'This isn't New Orleans,'" said Larry Bradshaw, a San Francisco paramedic who was among those fleeing.

Arthur Lawson, chief of the Gretna, La., Police Department, confirmed that his officers, along with those from the Jefferson Parish Sheriff's Office and the Crescent City Connection Police, sealed the bridge.

The New York Times, Sept 10, 2005, "Police in Suburbs Blocked Evacuees, Witnesses Report" by Gardiner Harris. © 2005 The New York Times Company. Reprinted with permission.

"There was no place for them to come on our side," Mr. Lawson said.

He said that he had been asked by reporters about officers threatening victims with guns or shooting over their heads, but he said that he had not yet asked his officers about that.

"As soon as things calm down, we will do an inquiry and find out what happened," he said.

The lawlessness that erupted in New Orleans soon after the hurricane terrified officials throughout Louisiana, and even a week later, law enforcement officers rarely entered the city without heavy weaponry.

While police officers saved countless lives and provided security to medical providers, many victims have complained bitterly about the behavior of some of the police officers in New Orleans in the days following Hurricane Katrina.

Officials in Lafayette, La., reported seeing scores of cruisers from the New Orleans police department in their city in the week after the hurricane. Some evacuees who fled to the Superdome and the convention center say that many police officers refused to patrol those structures after dark.

"It's unbelievable what the police officers did; they just left us," said Harold Veasey, a 66-year-old New Orleans resident who spent two horrific days at the convention center. And in the week after the hurricane, there were persistent rumors in and around New Orleans that police officers in suburban areas refused to help the storm victims.

Mr. Bradshaw and his partner, Lorrie Beth Slonsky, wrote an account about their experiences that has been widely circulated by e-mail and was first printed in *The Socialist Worker*.

Cathey Golden, a 51-year-old from Boston, and her 13-year-old son, Ramon Golden, yesterday confirmed the account.

The four met at the Hotel Monteleone in the French Quarter. Mr. Bradshaw and Ms. Slonsky had attended a convention for emergency medicine specialists. Ms. Golden and her two children, including 23-year-old Rashida Golden, were there to visit family.

The hotel allowed its guests and nearly 250 residents from the nearby neighborhood to stay until Thursday, Sept 1. With its food exhausted, the hotel's manager finally instructed people to leave. Hotel staff handed out maps to show the way to the city's convention center, to which thousands of other evacuees had fled.

A group of nearly 200 guests gathered to make their way to the center together, the four said. But on the way, they heard that the convention center had become a dangerous, unsanitary pit from which no one was being evacuated. So they stopped in front of a New Orleans police command post near the Harrah's casino on Canal Street.

A New Orleans police commander whom none of the four could identify told the crowd that they could not stay there and later told them that buses were being brought to the Crescent City Connection, a nearby bridge to Jefferson Parish, to carry them to safety.

The crowd cheered and began to move. Suspicious, Mr. Bradshaw said that he asked the commander if he was sure that buses would be there for them. "We'd had so much misinformation by that point," Mr. Bradshaw said.

"He looked all of us in the eye and said, 'I swear to you, there are buses waiting across the bridge,'" Mr. Bradshaw said.

But on the bridge there were four police cruisers parked across some lanes. Between six and eight officers stood with shotguns in their hands, the witnesses said. As the crowd approached, the officers shot over the heads of the crowd, most of whom retreated immediately, Mr. Bradshaw, Ms. Slonsky and Ms. Golden and her son said.

Mr. Bradshaw said the officers were allowing cars to cross the bridge, some of them loaded with passengers. Only pedestrians were being stopped, he said. Chief Lawson said he believed that only emergency vehicles were allowed through.

Mr. Bradshaw said he approached the officers and begged to be allowed through, saying a commander in New Orleans had told them buses were waiting for them on the other side.

"He said that there are no buses and that there is no foot traffic allowed across the bridge," Mr. Bradshaw said.

The remaining evacuees first sought refuge under a nearby highway overpass and then trudged back to New Orleans.

4

Police Begin Seizing Guns of Civilians

Alex Berenson and John M. Broder

Local police officers began confiscating weapons from civilians in preparation for a forced evacuation of the last holdouts still living here, as President Bush steeled the nation for the grisly scenes of recovering the dead that will unfold in coming days.

Police officers and federal law enforcement agents scoured the city carrying assault rifles seeking residents who have holed up to avoid forcible eviction, as well as those who are still considering evacuating voluntarily to escape the city's putrid waters.

"Individuals are at risk of dying," said P. Edwin Compass III, the superintendent of the New Orleans police. "There's nothing more important than the preservation of human life."

Although it appeared Wednesday night that forced evacuations were beginning, on Thursday the authorities were still looking for those willing to leave voluntarily. The police said that the search was about 80 percent done, and that afterward they would begin enforcing Mayor C. Ray Nagin's order to remove residents by force.

Mr. Bush, in Washington, urged the nearly one million people displaced by the storm to contact federal agencies to apply for immediate aid. He praised the outpouring of private charity to the displaced, but said the costs of restoring lives would affect all Americans, as would the horror of the storm's carnage.

"The responsibility of caring for hundreds of thousands of citizens who no longer have homes is going to place many demands on our nation," the president said in the Eisenhower Executive Office Building. "We have many difficult days ahead, especially as we recover those who did not survive the storm."

As Mr. Bush spoke, Vice President Dick Cheney was touring Mississippi and Louisiana, in part as an answer to the critics who have said that the administration responded too slowly and timidly to the epic disaster. At a stop in Gulfport, Miss., a heckler shouted an obscenity at the vice president. Mr. Cheney shrugged it off, saying it was the first such abuse he had heard.

Also on Thursday, Congress approved a $51.8 billion package of storm aid, bringing the total to more than $62 billion in a week. The government is now spending $2 billion dollars a day to respond to the disaster.

The confirmed death toll in Louisiana remained at 83 on Thursday. Efforts to recover corpses are beginning, although only a handful of bodies have been recovered so far. Official estimates of the death toll in New Orleans are still vague, but 10,000 remains a common figure.

Mississippi officials said they had confirmed 196 dead as of Thursday, including 143 in coastal areas, although Gov. Haley Barbour said he expected the toll to rise.

"It would just be a guess, but the 200 or just over 300 we think is a credible and reliable figure," the governor said on NBC's "Today" show.

He also said electricity would be restored by Sunday to most homes and businesses in the state that could receive it.

No one would venture a prediction about when the lights would come back on in New Orleans.

The water continued to recede slowly in the city 10 days after Hurricane Katrina swept ashore and levees failed at several points, inundating the basin New Orleans sits in.

The Army Corps of Engineers has restored to operation 37 of the city's 174 permanent pumps, allowing them to drain 11,000 cubic feet of water per second from the basin. When all the pumps are working, they can remove 81,000 cubic feet of water per second, said Dan Hitchings of the engineering corps.

It will be months before the breadth of the devastation from the storm is known. But a report by the Louisiana fisheries department calculated the economic loss to the state's important seafood industry at as much as $1.6 billion over the next 12 months.

Louisiana's insurance commissioner, J. Robert Wooley, said the state had barred insurance companies from canceling any homeowner's insurance policies in the days immediately before the storm hit and afterward.

"All cancellations will be voided," Mr. Wooley said.

Across New Orleans, active-duty soldiers, National Guard members and local law enforcement agencies from across the country continued door-to-door searches by patrol car, Humvee, helicopter and boat, urging remaining residents to leave.

Maj. Gen. James Ron Mason of the Kansas National Guard, who commands about 25,000 Guard troops in and around New Orleans, said his forces had rescued 687 residents by helicopter, boat and high-wheeled truck in the past 24 hours.

General Mason said Guard troops, although carrying M-16 rifles, would not use force to evict recalcitrant citizens. That, he said, was a job for the police, not members of the Guard.

"I don't believe that you will see National Guard soldiers actually physically forcing people to leave," General Mason said.

Mr. Compass, the police superintendent, said that after a week of near anarchy in the city, no civilians in New Orleans will be allowed to carry pistols, shotguns, or other firearms of any kind. "Only law enforcement are allowed to have weapons," he said.

That order apparently does not apply to the hundreds of security guards whom businesses and some wealthy individuals have hired to protect their property. The guards, who are civilians working for private security firms like Blackwater, are openly carrying M-16s and other assault rifles.

Mr. Compass said that he was aware of the private guards but that the police had no plans to make them give up their weapons.

New Orleans has turned into an armed camp, patrolled by thousands of local, state, and federal law enforcement officers, as well as National Guard troops and active-duty soldiers. While armed looters roamed unchecked last week, the city is now calm.

The city's slow recovery is continuing on other fronts as well, local officials said at a late morning news conference. Pumping stations are now operating across much of the city, and many taps and fire hydrants have water pressure. Tests have shown no evidence of cholera or other dangerous diseases in flooded areas.

With pumps running and the weather here remaining hot and dry, water has visibly receded across much of the city. Formerly flooded streets are now passable, although covered with leaves, tree branches and mud.

Still, many neighborhoods in the northern half of New Orleans remain under 10 feet of water, and Mr. Compass said Thursday that the city's plans for a forced evacuation remained in effect because of the danger of disease and fires.

Mr. Compass said he could not disclose when residents might be forced to leave en masse. The city's police department and federal law enforcement officers from agencies like United States Marshals Service will lead the evacuation, he said. Officers will search houses in both dry and flooded neighborhoods, and no one will be allowed to stay, he said.

Many of the residents still in the city said they did not understand why the city remained intent on forcing them out.

5

New Orleans Police Kill 4 in Shootout

Michael Luo

New Orleans police officers yesterday shot and killed four people and wounded two others who had fired at officers escorting a convoy of contractors across a bridge, the authorities said.

The group of 14 contractors from Boh Brothers Construction, one of New Orleans's largest construction companies, was working for the Army Corps of Engineers on levee repairs and drainage, said Robert Boh, the president of the company.

The convoy, which included officials from the Army Corps of Engineers and was being escorted by a group of police officers on an anti-looting detail, was crossing the Danziger Bridge, 10 miles northeast of the French Quarter, when the shots were fired.

W.J. Riley, the assistant superintendent of police in New Orleans, said a gunfight ensued between the police and a group of six men.

"All our officers said the assailants all had guns," Mr. Riley said. Later, he said all the assailants were "neighborhood thugs."

"Five of the subjects were shot," he said. "Two were killed, three were wounded." The sixth gunman was arrested and charged with attempted murder of a police officer, but none of the gunmen were identified.

The superintendent said that as the shooting broke out, two of the men fled across the bridge and were pursued by officers.

"One officer saw one subject go into a building," he said. "Another ran around the building. Shots were fired." Mr. Riley said one of the two was killed and the other was arrested.

None of the contractors were hurt and they were even initially unaware that anyone had been shot, said Mr. Boh, learning of it only later in news reports on the Internet.

6

New Orleans Sending In More Police to Stem Tide of Looting

NEW ORLEANS, Aug 31, 2005 (Dow Jones Commodities News Select via Comtex)—Looting broke out in some New Orleans neighborhoods, prompting authorities to send more than 70 additional officers and an armed personnel carrier into the city.

One police officer was shot in the head by a looter on Tuesday but was expected to recover, authorities said.

A giant new Wal-Mart (WMT) store in New Orleans was looted, and the entire gun collection was taken, *The Times-Picayune* reported. "There are gangs of armed men in the city moving around the city," said Ebbert, the city's homeland security chief. Also, looters tried to break into Children's Hospital, the governor's office said.

On New Orleans' Canal Street, dozens of looters ripped open the steel gates on clothing and jewelry stores and grabbed merchandise. In Biloxi, Miss., people picked through casino slot machines for coins and ransacked other businesses. In some cases, the looting was taking place in full view of police and National Guardsmen.

Louisiana Gov. Kathleen Blanco acknowledged that looting was a severe problem but said that officials had to focus on survivors. "We don't like looters one bit, but first and foremost is search and rescue," she said.

FWN Select, August 31, 2005 "New Orleans Sending In More Police to Stem Tide of Looting." © 2005 News provided by Comtex. © 2005 Dow Jones & Company, Inc. Reprinted with permission.

7

Midwest Police Face Trouble with Traffic, Not Looting

Adam Liptak

The widespread power blackout offered a challenge to police departments across the Midwest, which had to contend with snarled traffic, answer false calls from security alarms on the blink, and keep order at gas stations where desperate motorists tried to fill their tanks.

In several cities in the region, however, the police said they had not seen much looting or similar opportunistic crimes.

"How do you keep the populace reassured about government services in an emergency?" asked Daniel J. Oates, the police chief in Ann Arbor, Mich. "You saturate the community with police presence. You have police cars drive around with their lights on. We tripled the number of cops on the street last night. It cost me $10,000 in overtime."

In Melvindale, Mich., there were also no reports of major mayhem. "Everybody behaved well last night," said Lt. Rick Cadez of the police department there.

That is not to say everything went smoothly.

An explosion at an oil refinery in Melvindale, near Detroit, required the evacuation of more than 1,000 people there, Lieutenant Cadez said. The explosion was apparently linked to the power failure.

People were back in their homes by yesterday afternoon, after police and fire officials determined that the site was safe. There were no serious injuries.

Sgt. Ramona Bennett, a spokeswoman for the Detroit Police Department, said 88 major crimes and 25 arrests were reported during the first night of the blackout. "That's almost normal," she said.

The department has mobilized more than 200 volunteer reserve police officers to help patrol the streets, she said.

In Ann Arbor, the big problem was how to handle rush-hour traffic without traffic lights.

"The lights went out at about 4:15," Chief Oates said. "The traffic was absolutely chaotic immediately." Traffic was controlled at the half-dozen main intersections. "We got everybody out of town in about two and a half hours," he said, "and it's been great ever since."

Chief Oates said the power failures also set off various kinds of alarms. "They all have to be checked out eventually," he said.

Chief Oates did point to one incident that he said probably would not have happened on an ordinary night. Someone spray-painted anti-Semitic obscenities and a swastika on a Jewish student center at the University of Michigan, the first such incident in the chief's two years there.

Mark Wesley, a spokesman for the emergency management division of the Michigan State Police, said there had been isolated instances of looting in Detroit. He said the priorities of the state police were elsewhere.

"Our main focus is to provide water and energy," he said. "We want to make sure that the residents have adequate drinking water," he said, noting that the power had gone out at some water pumping stations.

"We also need to make sure we supply generators to critical facilities" like hospitals, he said.

He said both efforts were going well, though he noted that power might not be restored around Detroit until late in the weekend.

That might mean two more very dark nights, and they might turn stormy.

"We're also concerned about severe weather advisories," he added. "We have enough to handle as is."

The State Police have also assisted in ensuring that gasoline is available in Detroit, aided by an emergency suspension of rules about transporting and dispensing it that Gov. Jennifer M. Granholm issued early yesterday afternoon.

The blackout was less severe in Ohio than Michigan, and police officers there said their resources had not been severely taxed.

Youngstown, for instance, did not lose power but faced the threat of rolling blackouts, Capt. Jimmy Hughes said.

In Akron, Sgt. Dennis Woodall said the blackout had lasted just five hours. About 80 percent of the street lights went out, he said, but there were no major accidents or fires.

"We were in good shape," Sergeant Woodall said. "We were more concerned with people who had breathing difficulties in terms of the heat." No one, he said, died of a heat-related illness.

Fuel is a problem in Ohio. Sgt. Rick Zwayer of the Ohio State Highway Patrol said finding gasoline had been challenging for some drivers and the patrol had assisted a number of people whose cars had run out of gas.

Chief Oates, of Ann Arbor, reflected on the larger lessons of the blackout. "It just makes you appreciate electricity," he said. "We've got it bad, but think about Baghdad, where they've been without it off and on for months."

II

DEALING WITH SCAM-ARTISTS

The United States is known for its generosity during times of crisis. Donations pour in only days after a disaster hits. Government relief funds, charitable financial aid, and volunteers are intended to get people back on their feet as quickly as possible. But this assistance must reach the needy quickly. Unfortunately, swindlers, thieves, and con artists have discovered easy ways of enriching themselves illegally by taking advantage of desperate times and generous people. These criminals do not just take from the victims but also tie up police resources needed to investigate their frauds.

8

Hurricane Fraud Cases Surprise Even Officials

Eric Lipton

There is the Louisiana woman who reportedly used her aunt's New Orleans address and her brother's name to file a false claim for federal aid for Hurricane Katrina.

There are the Red Cross contract workers in California who are accused of cashing in on benefits for fictitious hurricane victims. And there are the two Florida residents who turned to the government for help, citing two hurricane-damaged houses in Slidell, La., that investigators say do not exist.

More than a month after the hurricane devastated the Gulf Coast, evidence is mounting that cheaters across the nation are trying to cash in on the catastrophe with a boldness that surprises even some longtime law enforcement officials.

"It is just amazing to me the moral values that seem to exist," said McGregor W. Scott, the United States attorney in Fresno, Calif., where nine area residents have been charged with defrauding the American Red Cross in a case involving false claims submitted to a Red Cross call center in Bakersfield, Calif.

The first scams involved fraudulent fund-raising, including fake Internet charities like AirKatrina.com, run by a Florida man who claimed to be piloting flights to Louisiana to provide emergency medical supplies.

"I saw dogs wrapped in electrical lines still alive and sparks flying from their bodies being electrocuted, as well as some people dead already," the pilot, Gary S. Kraser of Aventura, Fla., wrote in a pitch that helped raise almost $40,000 from 48 people. He has been charged with four counts of wire fraud.

The fraudulent acts now include people charged with trying to collect charity or government aid.

John Phillip Dugan, 19, of Baton Rouge, La., filed a claim using a false address and admitted to federal investigators that he intended to use the $2,000 in federal aid to pay for car repairs, a complaint filed against him said.

Barney Spears, 38, of Houston, and Nakia Grimes, 30, of Atlanta, separately claimed to be New Orleans residents in applying for federal aid, but investigators found that they lived hundreds of miles away, according to criminal complaints.

Veronica Jaeger, 22, and Kenneth M. Hodge, 33, both of Florida, separately claimed to live in houses in Slidell that a review by federal authorities says did not exist.

In Bakersfield, Red Cross staff members hired through a contractor created fake hurricane victims and issued checks on their behalf that the workers cashed or passed to friends or relatives, investigators say. The plot was detected, officials added, after the Red Cross noticed an unusually large number of money orders being sent to the area around its call center. Nine people have been charged on claims totaling $25,000. Mr. Scott said the numbers would most likely increase.

"You have got the Katrina victims who have been completely traumatized," he said. "And you have good-hearted American people reaching out trying to help their fellow citizens at a time of need."

The Justice Department has filed cases against 15 individuals. Local officials in Houston and other cities have filed charges in at least 50 cases. Hundreds of other cases are being reviewed, including more than 300 involving the Red Cross, a spokeswoman for the organization said.

The number represents a tiny share of the more than 2.2 million households that have applied for aid from the Federal Emergency Management Agency or the Red Cross and that are collecting $2.44 billion in federal aid and $854 million from the Red Cross, officials say.

Because of the enormous amount of aid money and the history of fraud after past catastrophes like the Sept. 11 attacks and the hurricanes in Florida last year, the Justice Department and the Homeland Security Department, which oversees the Federal Emergency Management Agency, set up special teams to investigate crimes related to Hurricane Katrina.

"We are not only going to punish it when it does happen," said Alice S. Fisher, assistant attorney general of the criminal division, who leads a special Katrina Fraud Task Force the Justice Department has established. "We are going to try to prevent it."

Congress has added $15 million for the inspector general of the Homeland Security Department to conduct the investigations, as well as others on hurricane relief contractors.

The President's Council on Integrity and Efficiency, made up of inspectors general, recommends allocating $45 million, enough to pay for 300 auditors and investigators.

Police officials in Houston have been aggressive. The Police Department sent undercover officers to a relief center to pose as victims and aid workers. The investigation found people who were bragging about applying repeatedly for one-time grants or who submitted fake identifications or addresses in an effort to obtain aid.

"Obviously, I am sure that a few got through," a spokesman for the police, Sgt. Nate McDuell, said. "We only wish there were more arrests."

9

After the Storm, the Swindlers

Tom Zeller Jr.

E ven as millions of Americans rally to make donations to the victims of
Hurricane Katrina, the Internet is brimming with swindles, come-ons
and opportunistic pandering related to the relief effort in Louisiana, Mississippi and Alabama. And the frauds are more varied and more numerous than
in past disasters, according to law enforcement officials and online watchdog
groups.

Florida's attorney general has already filed a fraud lawsuit against a man
who started one of the earliest networks of Web sites—katrinahelp.com,
katrinadonations.com and others—that stated they were collecting donations
for storm victims.

In Missouri, a much wider constellation of Internet sites—with names
like parishdonations.com and katrinafamilies.com—displayed pictures of the
flood-ravaged South and drove traffic to a single site, InternetDonations.org, a
nonprofit entity with apparent links to white separatist groups.

The registrant of those Web sites was sued by the state of Missouri yesterday for violating state fund-raising law and for "omitting the material fact that
the ultimate company behind the defendants' Web sites supports white
supremacy."

Late yesterday afternoon, the Federal Bureau of Investigation put the
number of Web sites claiming to deal in Katrina information and relief—some
legitimate, others not—at "2,300 and rising." Dozens of suspicious sites claiming links to legitimate charities are being investigated by state and federal

The New York Times, Sept 8, 2005, "After the Storm, the Swindlers" by Tom Zeller Jr.
© 2005 The New York Times Company. Reprinted with permission.

authorities. Also under investigation are e-mail spam campaigns using the hurricane as a hook to lure victims to reveal credit card numbers to thieves, as well as fake hurricane news sites and e-mail "updates" that carry malicious code aimed at hijacking a victim's computer.

"The numbers are still going up," said Dan Larkin, the chief of the Internet Crime Complaint Center operated by the F.B.I. in West Virginia. He said that the amount of suspicious, disaster-related Web activity was higher than the number of swindles seen online after last year's tsunami in Southeast Asia. "We've got a much higher volume of sites popping up," he said.

The earliest online frauds began to appear within hours of Katrina's passing. "It was so fast it was amazing," said Audri Lanford, co-director of ScamBusters.org, an Internet clearinghouse for information on various forms of online fraud. "The most interesting thing is the scope," she said. "We do get a very good feel for the quantity of scams that are out there, and there's no question that this is huge compared to the tsunami."

By the end of last week, Ms. Landford's group had logged dozens of Katrina-related swindles and spam schemes. The frauds ranged from opportunistic marketing (one spam message offered updates on the post-hurricane situation, with a link that led to a site peddling Viagra) to messages said to be from victims, or families of victims.

"This letter is in request for any help that you can give," reads one crude message that was widely distributed online. "My brother and his family have lost everything they have and come to live with me while they looks for a new job."

Several antivirus software companies have warned of e-mail "hurricane news updates" that lure users to Web sites capable of infecting computers with a virus that allows hackers to gain control of their machines. And numerous swindlers have seeded the Internet with e-mail "phishing" messages that say they are from real relief agencies, taking recipients to what appear to be legitimate Web sites, where credit card information is collected from unwitting victims who think they are donating to hurricane relief.

On Sunday, the Internet security company Websense issued an alert regarding a phishing campaign that lured users to a Web site in Brazil that was made to look like a page operated by the Red Cross. Users who submitted their credit card numbers, expiration dates and personal identification numbers via the Web form were then redirected to the legitimate Red Cross Web site, making the ruse difficult to detect. The security company Sophos warned of a similar phishing campaign on Monday.

"They're tugging at people's heartstrings," said Tom Mazur, a spokesman for the United States Secret Service. Mr. Mazur said there were "a number of instances that we're looking into with this type of fraud, both domestically and overseas," but he would not provide specifics.

The lawsuit filed in Florida last Friday accused Robert E. Moneyhan, a 51-year-old resident of Yulee, Fla., of registering several Katrina-related domain names—including KatrinaHelp.com, KatrinaDonations.com,

KatrinaRelief.com and KatrinaReliefFund.com—as early as Aug. 28, even before the hurricane had hit the Louisiana coast.

By Aug. 31, according to the Florida attorney general, Charles J. Crist Jr., Mr. Moneyhan's sites had begun asking visitors to "share your good fortune with Hurricane Katrina's victims." A "Donate" button then took payments through a PayPal account that Mr. Moneyhan had set up.

Mr. Moneyhan did not respond to numerous phone calls and e-mail messages, but the Web site names in question are now owned by ProjectCare.com, a loose collection of Web sites that is using the Katrina sites as an information center for hurricane victims.

Kevin Caruso, the proprietor of ProjectCare.com, said that he had offered to buy the sites from Mr. Moneyhan on Sept. 2, but that Mr. Moneyhan, distressed over the lawsuit, simply donated them to Project Care without charge. Mr. Caruso also said that after several phone conversations, he believed that Mr. Moneyhan, was "trying to help the Hurricane Katrina survivors, but did not have the experience to proceed properly."

The lawsuit, however, states that Mr. Moneyhan had tried to sell his collection of Katrina-related domain names on Sept. 1 "to the highest bidder." The suit seeks $10,000 in civil penalties and restitution for any consumers who might have donated to the Web sites while they were controlled by Mr. Moneyhan.

Jay Nixon, the Missouri attorney general, sued to shut one of the more bizarre fund-raising efforts yesterday. A state circuit court granted a temporary restraining order against Internet Donations Inc., the entity behind a dozen Web sites erected over the last several days purporting to collect donations for victims of Hurricane Katrina.

Also named in the Missouri suit, which seeks monetary penalties from the defendants, is the apparent operator of the donation sites, Frank Weltner, a St. Louis resident and radio talk show personality who operates a Web site called JewWatch.com.

That site—which indexes Adolf Hitler's writings, transcripts of anti-Semitic radio broadcasts and other materials, according to the Anti-Defamation League—attracted headlines last year when it appeared at or near the top of Google search results for the query "Jew." It remains the No. 2 search result today.

Most of Mr. Weltner's Katrina-related Web sites—which include KatrinaFamilies.com, Katrina-Donations.com, and NewOrleansCharities.com—appear to have been registered using DomainsByProxy.com, which masks the identity of a domain registrant.

However, Mr. Weltner's name appeared on public documents obtained through the Web site of the Missouri secretary of state yesterday. Those indicated that Mr. Weltner had incorporated Internet Donations as a nonprofit entity last Friday.

The various Web sites, which use similar imagery and slight variations on the same crude design, all point back to InternetDonations.org. There, visitors interested in donating to the Red Cross, Salvation Army or other relief organizations are told that "we can collect it for you in an easy one-stop location."

It is unclear whether any of the sites successfully drew funds from any donors, or if Mr. Weltner, who did not respond to e-mail messages and could not be reached by phone, had channeled any proceeds to the better-known charities named on his site. But the restraining order issued yesterday enjoins Mr. Weltner and Internet Donations Inc. from, among other things, charitable fund-raising in Missouri, and "concealing, suppressing or omitting" the fact that donations collected were intended "for white victims only."

"It's the lowest of the low when someone solicits funds" this way, Mr. Nixon said in an interview before announcing the lawsuit. "We don't want one more penny from well-meaning donors going through this hater."

III

RESPONDING
TO RIOTS

Anarchistic in nature, a violent mob does not respond to authority or follow orders but creates its own dynamic unique to the situation and environment. When de-individualization sets in, people turn into followers who copy their leaders' acts without questioning them. Experience has shown that the mere presence of police officers in proper riot gear can trigger violence in emotionally charged demonstrators. Political extremists have also hijacked demonstrations and turned them into attacks on the establishment. Our police supervisors and officers are generally only trained to handle single incidents. Riot control, however, requires a synchronized police force that responds professionally and uniformly. Provocations must not be taken personally but in the context of the whole. Police strategies must be fine-tuned and constantly monitored to ensure that they do not interfere with the constitutional rights of the citizens.

10

In L.A., Trying to Keep a Lid on Racial Strife

Recent Killing of a Black Youth Stirs Tensions Between Police and Neighborhoods 13 Years After King Riots

Daniel B. Wood

At Leimert Park, a gathering place for demonstrations and rallies in south-central Los Angeles, the thunder of djembe drums adds a dramatic accompaniment to a long queue of local protest speakers. As each steps up to a microphone planted in the grass, their words seem to ring with echoes of an earlier violent era in the battle for civil rights.

"The time is now," yells one protestor to the crowd of about 350 holding placards and signs. "No more police terrorism."

The occasion, a community-wide gathering to protest the killing of a 13-year-old African-American youth by Los Angeles police, has become another major flashpoint in Los Angeles race relations. For several weeks, black leaders have held meetings and marches to draw attention to the shooting as evidence that the LAPD has not budged in its decades-old culture of riding herd over ethnic residents as adversaries rather than citizens to "serve and protect."

It's been more 10 years since the LAPD became the international poster child for dysfunctional policing—first in the Rodney King beating, then with two trials of O.J. Simpson. Now, the high-profile incident of Devin Brown—who was shot and killed by police when he refused orders to stop fleeing in a stolen car—once again raises the question of how much police reform, if any, has occurred since the largest riots in US history here raised public consciousness of the problem of police abuse.

Despite the anger in Leimert Park, there is some consensus that much improvement has been made throughout American police departments. Yet there is also consensus that the patterns of racist behavior exhibited by police have not been adequately addressed.

"You might say the policy, training, and equipment side of American policing has come a long way since Rodney King but that the human side, police interacting with residents, has come less far," says Mary Powers, director of the National Coalition on Police Accountability (NCOPA).

Accomplishments include policy changes regarding how and when to use force and in what form. They also include better cultural and sensitivity training, and community-based policing. All have brought more police into direct contact with the neighborhoods they serve.

In addition, more cities now have civilian committees with the leverage to formally hold police departments accountable for questionable actions.

NEGATIVE PERCEPTIONS PERSIST

At the same time, not enough has been accomplished to better police-community race relations, say experts. In this regard, they say, Los Angeles is a case in point for problems nationwide.

"I think racism is the problem here," says Mary Alice Jones of the Congress of Racial Equality. She points out that 83 percent of LAPD officers do not live within city limits and many appear to have had little exposure to racial diversity.

To her and others, the Devin Brown shooting is only one incident in a much larger pattern of negative police actions. Just four days prior to that shooting, officials here announced they would not prosecute a June incident in which a LAPD officer struck a car thief suspect 11 times with a flashlight. And in January, two white cops won a jury verdict of $2.4 million in a discrimination suit for being wrongly terminated following a 2002 beating of another black suspect.

BETTER POLICE TRAINING STILL NEEDED

But other observers say there simply has not been enough focus on police training in the specific area of emergency response. That means better understanding of the complexity of one's own reflexes and emotions when life or death decisions must be made in seconds.

Here in Los Angeles, Ms. Powers and others say, there are still deeply ingrained behaviors in the "police culture" that are strong enough to survive new chiefs of police, city council changes, and turnovers of mayors and oversight boards. Codes of silence, in which police officers refuse to rat on colleagues for wrongdoing, undermine efforts to establish accountability.

"You can pass all the policy guideline changes, have . . . blue ribbon commissions, [but] one thing that has not changed is the fundamental core component that courses through everything involving the LAPD: the violent, confrontational mentality of the LAPD," says Earl Ofari Hutchinson, author of several books on the African-American experience in US culture.

Despite widespread feelings that little improvement has been made in police-community relations here, several black leaders have defended the LAPD in the wake of the current shooting.

TANGIBLE PROGRESS NOTED

"It is absolutely incorrect that no progress has been made within the LAPD ranks," says Bernard Parks, an African-American city council member and the former LAPD chief. "Training has evolved, cultural sensitivity has evolved, accountability and discipline have evolved. You must realize that police officers are human beings in dynamic situations that may take someone's life. If anyone thinks there is perfectionism, they are going to be disappointed."

There are also African-Americans willing to point the finger at the actions of black perpetrators that have led to police confrontations. "Many in black neighborhoods . . . seem to forget that in every one of these run-ins with police . . . there has been at the core of the incident, an African-American breaking the law and resisting arrest," says Ted Hayes, who runs temporary housing for the homeless.

NCOPA's Mary Powers and other national observers also see progress. She points to three recent examples: a change in the shooting policy for officers regarding moving cars, the use of flashlights in beating suspects, and high-speed pursuits.

But many feel that an underlying culture of racism will continue to exacerbate the problem of police and community relations. "In the 1960s and '70s we were suing police departments all over the country insisting that if we changed the racial makeup of the police, we would end police brutality," says Ramona Ripston, director of the southern California chapter of ACLU. "Well, we did integrate them and guess what, it [police abuse] didn't change."

She and other experts here call for more stringent policies that require police to live in the communities they serve.

11

Public Risk Managers Reflect on Riots (PRIMA Conference Report)

Alfred G. Haggerty

Abstract: *The 1992 Los Angeles, CA, riots have caused municipal risk managers to reflect on city preparations for riot-control. Surveyed at the Public Risk Management Association 1992 annual conference, risk managers indicated that although there would generally be no major changes in risk management practices, improved coordination between various public agencies and the public could yield dividends. Little criticism of the handling of the riots by the Los Angeles Police Department was offered. It was felt concentrating efforts on stopping looting should not override attempts to limit injuries. Risk managers need to be more aware of the law enforcement environment.*

ANAHEIM, Calif.—One result of the recent rioting in Los Angeles may be an expanded role for public risk managers in helping cities to avoid similar outbreaks of civil commotion.

At the same time, some municipal risk managers are generally satisfied with their current procedures and the way they've handled potentially explosive situations in their jurisdictions.

These are some conclusions based on a series of interviews conducted by the National Underwriter here at the 13th annual Conference for Public

National Underwriter Property & Casualty-Risk & Benefits Management, May 25, 1992 n21, p3(2) "Public Risk Managers Reflect on Riots" by Alfred G. Haggerty. © National Underwriter Co. 1992. Reprinted with permission.

Agencies sponsored by the Arlington, Va.-based Public Risk Management Association.

Those queried offered little or no criticism of the efforts of the Los Angeles Police Department during the city's recent riots.

Thomas Vance, risk manager for the city of Anaheim, which sent 40 police officers and fire fighters to Los Angeles during the riots, said perhaps cities have a role to play in educating small business owners in the areas of insurance and risk management. He said he will recommend that Anaheim hold some classes, and that whether such classes become a reality all depends on whether the city wants to make the commitment.

Mr. Vance also said it may be the city's role to intercede and tell insurance underwriters that "things aren't as bad as they seem" and that the police and fire departments do a better job of protecting the community than they think.

Mr. Vance said he isn't sure he would agree with a statement by Richard Welch, risk manager for Los Angeles, that the city's risk management planning effort fell short in its preparations for looting during a riot. (See NU, May 18, page one.)

If all the police officers in Los Angeles had been arresting looters during the riots, Mr. Vance said, soon there would have been no police left on the street, because they would have been tied up processing those arrests.

He said it's "impossible" to say the L.A. police "did it wrong," adding that there might have been more damage if police had made a lot of arrests and been taken off the street to handle the prisoners.

He also noted the civil rights liability exposures police face in riots, adding that he isn't sure how much leeway local law enforcement has in bringing riots and civil commotion under control.

In one recent case, he said, police used a felt tip pen to write arrest numbers on members of a crowd arrested during a disturbance in order to facilitate the processing. He said people filed suit, claiming mental cruelty because the use of the felt tip pens to write numbers on the suspects was akin to the branding of prisoners in Nazi concentration camps.

"If you don't follow the rules, you open yourself to civil litigation. You have to look at the city as a corporation and protect the property of its citizens against lawsuits," Mr. Vance said. He said he's not sure what the Los Angeles police could have done that they didn't do.

Asked what he might do differently as a result of the L.A. riots, Mr. Vance said he only recommends training as it affects city liability and he doesn't get involved in police decisions. He said he places the safety of city employees, including police officers and fire fighters, over the safety of property.

Mr. Vance called the Los Angeles riots "a fortuitous event, the kind of thing that's meant to be covered by insurance" and is not necessarily avoidable.

Ron J. Guilfoile, risk manager for the city of St. Paul, Minn., said in large cities like St. Paul the risk manager's involvement with law enforcement is "pretty-minimal" and suggested that this situation should change. He said risk management is often better funded for police departments than for any other city department and "we've had a tendency to leave them alone."

"Maybe we have to get more involved," said Mr. Guilfoile, reflecting on the Los Angeles riots. He said he plans to meet more often with top city officials and the police chief in order to get better prepared. For example, he said, the Parks and Recreation Department could put on special programs to ease community tensions and warn police of such tensions.

"What happened in South-Central Los Angeles showed us the need for a multi-faceted attack on problems," Mr. Guilfoile said.

Aadne Benestad, risk manager for Sacramento County, Calif., said state and local police in his area handled the situation well in the hours and days following the Los Angeles riots, including the threat that the rioting would spread throughout the state.

Mr. Benestad attributed the lack of any major trouble in both the city and county of Sacramento largely to the increased use of community-type patrols. He said these patrols involve the regular assignment of officers to certain neighborhoods, enabling them to get to know the people and develop relationships with them. That type of preparation, he said, "has made a difference."

Last year, Mr. Benestad said, police work within the community helped avoid trouble following a hostage situation in an electronics store in Sacramento in which three of the four hostage-takers, all members of minorities, were killed.

"Some people criticized the sheriff," he said, "but nothing has happened." He said they felt the police had "done everything possible."

Coincidentally, PRIMA responded to the concern generated by the L.A. riots with the release of a new book: "Risk Management Behind the Blue Curtain: A Primer on Law Enforcement Liability." PRIMA said the book was written to help risk managers understand the law enforcement environment.

Chapters outline a six-layered liability protection system, the legal basis for civil liability, the need for police training, the exposure to liability during police pursuit and a recommendation for a plan for action by risk managers. The author is G. Patrick Gallagher, director of the Institute for Liability Management of Leesburg, Va.

12

More Risk Management Urged for L.A. Cops

City Risk Mgr. Thinks Risk Awareness Leads to Cooler Approach (Richard Welch; Los Angeles, California)

David M. Katz

Abstract: *Richard Welch, city risk manager for Los Angeles, CA, says risk manage-ment should be high-priority for the LA Police Dept since liability claims from police action cost the city $25–$35 million each year. Emergency planning for the police department in LA is confidential, so risk managers are not privy to many of the details and planning centers on natural disaster emergencies. During the 1992 riots there was no control of looting and no protection for emergency service personnel. Hopes are pinned on new police chief Willie Williams, whose community-based policing tactics are expected to be more appropriate for handling such situations.*

The city risk manager for Los Angeles feels that risk management should play a greater role in the emergency planning operations of the Los Angeles police and that an increased awareness by police of the potential liabilities of their acts might lead to a "less confrontational" atmosphere in the city's communities, he said in an exclusive interview following the recent Los Angeles riots.

Because the police department's emergency tactical planning is, unlike those of other city departments, confidential, Los Angeles' three risk managers have less of a role in emergency planning in the police department than they do in other departments, Richard Welch told the National Underwriter.

National Underwriter Property & Casualty-Risk & Benefits Management, May 18, 1992 n20 p1(2) "More Risk Management Urged for L.A. Cops: City Risk Mgr. Thinks Risk Awareness Leads to Cooler Approach (Richard Welch; Los Angeles, California)" by David M. Katz. © National Underwriter Co. 1992. Reprinted with permission.

"If I had my way, I'd like to see them consider risk management as one of the most important aspects" of their organization, he said, nothing that "the preponderance" of the $25 million to $35 million in liability claims the city spends annually stems from police activity.

While "you can't really second-guess" the actions police take during a riot, "if they had an awareness of third-party liability claims [it] might make a difference in how they respond in a situation," he said, noting that the response might be "less confrontational." (See NU editorial, page 26.)

Mr. Welch said he hoped that the approach of incoming police chief Willie Williams, which emphasizes more community-based policing, "will minimize problems in a riot situation." (Community-based policing emphasizes police officers walking a beat instead of cruising areas in patrol cars.)

Such an approach could counter the image of "a distant uniformed force that only shows up when it has trouble" to deal with, the risk manager said.

While Los Angeles officials tend to think of the city "as one of the best" in terms of emergency planning, "most of our planning is for natural disasters," he said.

The planning effort fell short in its preparations for looting during a riot and the protection of firefighters from rioters, according to Mr. Welch, who assessed the lessons of the riots, provided structural insights into how risk management works in the city and supplied riot damage information in the interview.

"In planning sessions of the last few years, we haven't given enough attention to looting," he said, noting "what a tremendous strain that is" on police riot operations.

Citing live television coverage of the riots which showed "whole families breaking into stores and hauling off . . . large quantities of merchandise," Mr. Welch said that "if you send police to guard those stores, they can't respond to fighting."

During the riots "there were many instances of looting where there was no police protection," he said.

The situation was "exacerbated by media coverage which said, Here we are at the corner of such and such, where there are no police," he added.

Another area in which emergency planning was inadequate was the anticipation of hostility to firefighters, according to Mr. Welch.

"It seems ironic that people would attack firefighters. But that was what happened," he said, noting that local residents in the riot area attacked one firefighter with an ax and shot another in the face.

Protection for firefighters "probably wasn't given as much weight as, in retrospect, it should have been," he said.

On the other hand, one positive element in the city's preparedness for the riots was the fact that the fire department had a longstanding "mutual aid agreement" with Los Angeles County and with other neighboring cities, Mr. Welch said.

"Those other jurisdictions were able to respond immediately [to fires ignited during the riots] because of the contingency plans that are laid out," he said, noting that the agreement also includes personnel and equipment support.

When the riots began, the city's Emergency Operations Organization, located four stories under city-owned land, was activated, as it is during disasters or other emergencies, according to Mr. Welch.

In addition to emergency police and fire department telephone operators, members of the Emergency Operations Organization, which includes representatives of such major departments as fire, police, public works and building, worked out of the control center, according to Mr. Welch.

Also represented in the organization is the City Administrative Officer (CAO), to whom Mr. Welch reports, the risk manager said.

Mr. Welch said that in general he, along with two other officials who have the title of risk manager, provide technical advice to the managers of 33 city departments.

While the riots were in progress, Mr. Welch, who is responsible for property-casualty insurance and self-insurance, provided advice to the CAO's own emergency staff on such matters as what city properties were affected and what kind of coverage was in place, he said.

In fact, Los Angeles is, except for some dedicated self-insurance funds and property coverage, "legally uninsured," he said. "We pay losses out of our ordinary operating budget. We're the typical pay-as-you-go city."

The city, however, does have commercial physical damage insurance on buildings financed with bonds, he said. As of the May 7 interview, none of those buildings appeared to be damaged, he added.

While the Los Angeles convention center, which has some property-casualty insurance (and is self-insured for earthquakes) is in an area that sustained some riot damage, it went undamaged, according to Mr. Welch.

Overall, the amount of direct damage to city-owned property, which included broken windows and a parking-attendant kiosk that was burned, was "relatively small," he said, noting that the worst of the damage struck private-sector buildings in South-Central Los Angeles.

"We have sustained rough estimates of $3.3 million in direct property damage in departments the city Council controls," he said, adding that damage estimates incurred by the city's harbor, airport and water and power departments were excluded from that figure.

The damage estimate included about $800,000 incurred from the loss of the contents of two branch libraries burned during the riots, according to Mr. Welch. Since Los Angeles had leased the library buildings, the loss of the structures themselves was not included in the city's damage estimate, he said.

The city's water department reported $8.5 million in damages—mostly downed power lines and transmission equipment, he said.

As of the day of the interview, there had been no liability claims filed against the city, he said, adding that any which are filed would be handled by the city attorney's office.

Following the riots, there was "an intense focus on recovery efforts," Mr. Welch said. "A few days ago, we had spent $18 million in staffing and overtime [pay in connection with the riots]," he added, noting that much of that amount is recoverable from the Federal Emergency Management Agency.

Speaking of the role of risk management in Los Angeles' complex governmental structure, he said "we would like to have a stronger visibility . . . in all the operating departments."

In fact Mr. Welch chairs a risk management advisory committee which meets quarterly and includes senior staff representatives from the city's major operating departments, including public works, recreation, transportations and housing.

But in a "somewhat decentralized" organization like that of the Los Angeles government, with its 33 departments and the city's 484 square miles, achieving a higher profile is a hard task, he said.

"Any time you have so many layers of administration, it's hard to keep risk management in the forefront," Mr. Welch said.

13

Boston Faces
Riot-Control Test

A Student Was Killed Last Week as Police Tried to Curb Unruly Celebrations. Would a World Series Win Turn Violent?

Sara B. Miller

B OSTON—The city of the Fenway Faithful is buzzing with pent-up energy, the kind that may aid and abet a Red Sox triumph—or a riot in the streets.

As Boston reels with hope for its first World Series victory since 1918, residents and officials here are also grappling with difficult issues of mob control and public safety. Last week, the celebration after the Sox won their series slot, beating the Yankees in New York, turned deadly. Thousands of fans filled the streets near Fenway Park, and in the chaos a Emerson College student was hit in the eye by a police pepper-spray bullet. She died hours later.

The Boston Police department has been criticized for its role in the death, as it attempted to control a joyous crowd turned riotous. The resulting publicity is prompting debate about proper police response, and is shaping preparations for crowd control if the Sox win this week.

The death also highlights a challenge that goes beyond Boston: an unruly brand of sport celebration, especially among college-age males. The challenge is especially acute here, where the culture is ruled in equal measure by sports and academia. This city could be a test case for understanding why such a tribal response has become an almost automatic extension of tense playoff games.

"What's happening, and not just when there are losses, but when [the team] is victorious, fans torch cars, turn them over," says Leonard Zaichkowsky, a sport psychology expert at Boston University. Celebrations should be associated with joy and gratitude, but they too often transition into a hostility and destruction, he says.

This "mob mentality" isn't new. It was seen in Roman spectator riots in the 6th century. And Europe has long dealt with soccer "hooligans."

But in America, rioting has increasingly marred celebrations in professional and college sports.

Earlier this year after the New England Patriots won the Super Bowl, a 21-year-old was hit by a car in the rowdiness that erupted in Boston. Dozens of students were arrested for flipping cars and setting fires at the University of Connecticut when the men's and women's basketball teams won national championships last spring.

MAYOR'S AND POLICE RESPOND

Last week, with tens of thousands of fans in the streets here, some hurling garbage cans and throwing bottles at officers, police in riot gear tried to contain the chaos. The pepper bullets were not supposed to land above the shoulders, but one of them hit Victoria Snelgrove in the eye. The use of so-called nonlethal force in this case turned deadly. In a statement, Boston Police Commissioner Kathleen O'Toole took full responsibility for any errors on the part of the police and announced that an internal investigation would be opened.

She has also harshly condemned rioters, but the police will shift to lower-powered pellet guns.

Mayor Thomas Menino announced some broader steps to control crowds, including limits on the length of waiting lines outside sports bars and a ban on live broadcasts showing fans within. He also met with members of the university community "to prevent hooliganistic activity after victorious sporting events," says Seth Gitell, a spokesman for the mayor.

While there may not be a simple explanation for the psychology of rioting, the behavior does tend to fall within a certain demographic: white, male, and college-age. The violence usually begins with a small percentage of youths, and then the anonymity provided by crowds lends itself to a sinister version of "follow the leader."

Rob McCarter, a junior at Northeastern University, headed to Fenway Park with a couple of his friends as soon as the game ended Wednesday night. He wasn't scared, he says, despite the cops in helmets and jackets and the vandalism taking place around him. He says he got a laugh out of a group that hurled a dumpster into a bank window, but "I wasn't going to be one of those guys to break stuff."

MOBS: CAUSES AND SOLUTIONS

Society's acceptance of the rowdy, sometimes violent, element of sports allegiance is, in part, to blame. "Though it's antisocial, [the violence] is still a feat of skill," says Jerry Lewis, sociologist at Kent State University in Ohio. It's not unlike the skill that a football player exhibits on the field. "The identification with the team is expressed through these acts of violence."

Some see alcohol as a prime influence. In fact, Mayor Menino had considered invoking a state law allowing him to ban the sale or distribution of alcohol "in cases of riot or great public excitement."

The problem is not just alcohol, but a new brand of "extreme" drinking on campuses, say Brandon Busteed, founder of Outside the Classroom, which provides online alcohol prevention courses for students. When he was a student at Duke University, Mr. Busteed says, burning benches after basketball victories was the norm. He sought to provide alternative events in lieu of the alcohol-fueled vandalism that plagued Duke. Such sanctioned events immediately after sporting victories, say experts, could help cities counter rioting.

There is also a lack of public education, with no institution taking prime responsibility for education the public on the issue, says Professor Zaichkowsky. Is it the duty of the police? Team owners? The athletes? The city? "It falls through the cracks."

The Boston police have faced at least some criticism for use of pepper spray guns. Many say not enough study has proven that stun guns or other types of "nonlethal" weapons reduce death. "I think there really needs to be a national reassessment of this paramilitary force on citizens," says Paul Wertheimer of Crowd Management Strategies in Chicago. "This is not Fallujah."

Meanwhile, a dean at Boston University has notified students and their parents threatening expulsion if students engage in illegal behavior.

14

Police to Use
Containment Pens
to Handle Protest
on March 20

Shaila K. Dewan

The Police Department is denying a request to refrain from using inter-
locking metal barricades to contain demonstrators at a March 20 march
and rally, the organizers said yesterday.

Demonstrators, civil rights advocates and the police say they view the
protest, against the occupation of Iraq, as a test of how all sides will handle
demonstrations during the Republican National Convention.

The police said the pens would increase safety, help crosstown traffic flow,
and enable them to use fewer officers at big events. "It's not to create a hostile
environment," said Paul J. Browne, the chief spokesman for the department.

Protest organizers say the pens are more appropriate for controlling cattle
than people, and they point out that countless demonstrations in New York
and elsewhere have been held peaceably without them.

"They're very confusing for people," said Leslie Cagan, the national coor-
dinator for United for Peace and Justice, the organizers of the March 20 event.
Mr. Browne said that the pens, which would be closed one by one as they
fill with people, would be used only during the rally, not the march, and
that people would be allowed to leave at will. He said the department would

The New York Times, March 12, 2004, "Police to Use Containment Pens to Handle
Protest on March 20" by Shaila K. Dewan. © 2004 The New York Times Company.
Reprinted with permission.

post directions for protesters on its Web site. "While they're there they can go to our recruitment page if they're interested in joining the department," he deadpanned.

United for Peace and Justice was responsible for a major antiwar demonstration in February 2003 in which demonstrators complained that the police used charging horses, unprovoked arrests and a maze of barricades to control the crowd, preventing some people from leaving and blocking tens of thousands from reaching the demonstration site.

Police Commissioner Raymond W. Kelly gave the police high marks for its handling of that event, which was attended by more than 100,000 people. He blamed problems on a lack of cooperation from organizers, who he said failed to advertise the correct location or provide the promised number of marshals.

After that demonstration, the New York Civil Liberties Union filed suit to prevent the police from using perimeter barricades and pens, dispersing crowds with horses without notice, and searching demonstrators. The group's fears that the police will use the threat of arrest to discourage protesters were heightened this week when Robert M. Morgenthau, the Manhattan district attorney, said his office was told to expect 1,000 arrests a day at the convention.

"They should be figuring out how not to arrest 1,000 people, not how to arrest 1,000 people," said Christopher Dunn, the associate legal director of the civil liberties union.

The police and the demonstration organizers also disagreed yesterday about arrangements. Mr. Browne said demonstrators would enter Madison Avenue at 42nd Street and walk down to assemble for the march. Ms. Cagan said they were also telling people to approach from the north, but from 34th Street.

One issue, however, was resolved: unlike last year, the police agreed to allow portable toilets at the rally.

IV

DEALING WITH
THE TRAUMA

Anyone would agree that the job of police officers, firefighters, and paramedics can be extremely stressful. They are confronted with great human tragedies that often test their coping skills to the limit. Multiplied by hundreds or thousands, these traumatic events can push the response and rescue personnel past their physical and psychological brink. The following articles are accounts of the impact of such tragedies.

15

Scarred Police Force Tries to Regroup after Storm

David Heinzmann

Oct. 9—NEW ORLEANS—Like everything else in New Orleans, law enforcement has been turned upside down. The highest crime neighborhoods have been wiped off the map and replaced with rolling wastelands of mud, lumber and filth. The courthouse is in the train station, and most of the Police Department's office help was given pink slips last week.

Once one of the most violent cities in America, New Orleans is now mostly making arrests for curfew violations and petty drug offenses. The real dangers in New Orleans are sickness and despair wrought by Hurricane Katrina.

Against that backdrop, roughly 80 percent of the 1,450 police officers now working are homeless and living on a Carnival cruise ship leased by the federal government and docked on the Mississippi River. Humiliated by allegations that some of them deserted their posts during the storm, the exhausted and heartbroken rank and file now have grave anxieties about their futures as New Orleans cops.

Rumors abound about pay cuts, or even officer layoffs, and hundreds of officers will have to decide in the coming months whether to try to stay in this devastated city or relocate to build new lives with their families.

"We're basically just working day to day," Officer Roger Jones said one morning last week as he headed out after 7 a.m. roll call. "I have friends who have sent applications to different departments. A lot of the veterans say that, after the rebuilding, they're just going to leave."

More than 50 officers quit in the wake of the disaster, and the department is investigating 249 officers whose whereabouts and conduct during the first days of the storm have been questioned.

Although it must first determine how to police the redevelopment of a catastrophically damaged and unstable city, the NOPD's biggest challenge over the next year may be surviving its own instability. Interim Superintendent Warren Riley said one of his biggest concerns is preventing a slow, quiet drain of good officers over the coming months.

"That's a major problem for us right now, as it relates to housing our officers. That's going to be a problem for a long time," Riley said last week in an interview with the Chicago Tribune. "A lot of officers' families are settling in other cities. . . . So we will probably lose some officers because . . . the fact that you can't bring your family back home for a very long time will make it a difficult situation."

Policing in the wake of Hurricane Katrina would be terrifyingly uncharted territory for any big-city police department to navigate. But NOPD is also saddled with a checkered past and a reputation for corruption and inefficiency.

A decade ago, the department was rocked by corruption charges, including officers helping drug dealers murder rival gangsters. The force was purged of about 200 corrupt cops in the late 1990s, and leaders reorganized the way the department fights crime and how it oversees police conduct.

The force's reputation has improved in recent years, but the department is still struggling. Riley was appointed after the sudden resignation of his boss two weeks ago. And many of the 249 officers under investigation will likely be fired.

But cops here, and in the region, say NOPD has gotten a bad rap in the aftermath of Katrina.

After the levees broke and flooded the city, police officers "found themselves in a situation where they literally didn't have a place to stand and call headquarters," said Louisiana State Police Lt. Col. Joseph Booth. "Given what they went through, they've actually made a fairly quick recovery."

Riley said many of the officers who were unaccounted for in those early days were actually working—just not in their assigned districts. Many went to any district headquarters they could reach and then were cut off from communications with the rest of the department because radios and phones didn't work. Three of the city's eight district headquarters were under water, and officers working there were stranded for days.

And as Riley pointed out, many officers were victims of Katrina.

"We have over 80 officers we had to rescue off of roofs and out of attics," he said. "And some of them were there for three or four days."

Some cops reportedly took advantage of the chaos to loot merchandise. But Officer Jones said he viewed much of that behavior as necessary to survival.

Early on in the disaster, "I was in a grocery store and people were coming up to me and asking if they could take things. I said as long as it was basics, food and clothing, it was OK."

It was the same with cops, he said. Most needed clothes and food, and vehicles to function.

"Most of our cars were trashed," he said, so they commandeered vehicles that were still operative. "The first couple days, no one knew what was going on. We looked to headquarters for direction, but headquarters was in disarray itself."

Now that the water has receded, and officers have settled into the bizarre routine of living on a ship, the mood has changed from desperation to anxiety.

Mayor C. Ray Nagin laid off half of the city's workforce last Tuesday, but said police officers, firefighters and ambulance crews would be spared. But not all police officers are convinced. They fear the battering their reputation took in the first days could make them vulnerable when the city's fiscal problems get worse.

Riley has tried to set minds at ease about job security. The housing situation will remain up in the air for a long time, he said, but he believes the federal government won't leave New Orleans in the lurch with no means to pay cops and firefighters.

To adjust to the ravaged city's different needs, Riley created a 100-officer anti-looting squad, and reassigned everybody except a few detectives to work patrol. Ordinarily about 68 percent of sworn officers would be patrolling the city. Now, it's more like 92 percent, Riley said. And they're in different areas. Before the storm, the impoverished Lower Ninth Ward was the most troubled part of the city. But it is now a no-man's land of crushed houses and debris, its streets lost under tons of dried muck.

In a city that had more than 400,000 residents, there are now fewer than 100,000. Most are in neighborhoods that suffered less storm damage—such as Algiers on the west bank of the Mississippi.

"What we're really focusing on is, obviously, that the areas that are most populated will have a high visibility of police," Riley said. "We want to welcome our citizens and the contractors back into the city. We want to assure them they will be safe. And we will expect nothing but professionalism from our officers."

With so many empty neighborhoods, police have seen almost no violent crime since the initial chaos wrought by Katrina. But French Quarter nightlife began sloshing into Bourbon Street again last week and police found themselves cuffing drunken revelers. And every morning in a shabby, borrowed room at the train station, a judge sets bond for a handful of people hauled in for curfew and drug violations the night before.

Of the 21 suspects in bond court Wednesday morning before Judge Gerard Hansen, none was charged with violent crimes, and only one had been caught with a gun.

"There aren't enough people here to commit violent crime, and the people who commit violent crime are now elsewhere," Hansen said.

But crime problems more typical to New Orleans are beginning to reappear. At night, patrol cars creep through deserted neighborhoods plunged into utter darkness. Officers have caught criminals sneaking back into the city after curfew, either to loot or to retrieve drugs they stashed during the storm.

"Lots of people left their drugs and guns here, and it's still here," said Officer Roland Doucette, steering a borrowed pickup through the ruined Lower Ninth. He said police are seeing dealers racing each other back into dangerous areas to see who can find the stashes first.

Police have no idea how much of the hard-core drug and violent crime will return to New Orleans, but it is clearly going to be less of a concern for a while. Riley said he doesn't anticipate the city having a population of more than 200,000 for a long time.

Law enforcement officials say that would be helpful for dealing with all of the unknowns they face.

Jones said he was one of the lucky members of the force, because his list of uncertainties does not include a place to call home. His house in Algiers survived with minimal damage, and his wife and kids have not needed to relocate. Because of that, he said, there is no question that he'll be patrolling New Orleans streets—whatever they look like—for years to come.

"I have no intention of leaving," Jones said. "You couldn't drag me away."

16

With Some Now at Breaking Point, City's Officers Tell of Pain and Pressure

Joseph B. Treaster and John Desantis

Sgt. Jeff Sandoz, dressed in black SWAT team fatigues with an assault shotgun nearby, took a break on Monday afternoon for a cheeseburger, his first hot meal in a week, in the breezeway at the shuttered Harrah's casino on the edge of the French Quarter.

Rescuing people from rooftops and attics and chasing looters since Hurricane Katrina flooded the city, the discomforts have piled up, Sergeant Sandoz acknowledged. His shoulder was bruised on Wednesday when his police cruiser was rammed by someone running a stop sign on one of New Orleans's nearly deserted streets. He has been catching about three hours of sleep a night, curled up in the back seat of his patrol car, and showering with a garden hose.

He did not want to talk about the blisters or funguses and rashes that have erupted—after days of wading in polluted water in wet boots and dirty socks—on the feet of most everyone in the eight-man tactical unit he commands.

The last week has been a series of nonstop rescue missions, shootouts in the night and forays into foul-smelling shelters in response to gunshots and reports of rape for Sergeant Sandoz and the others on the New Orleans police force. And like most everyone else in New Orleans, police officers have been traumatized by the loss of homes and family members.

Morale on the police force is in tatters. About 500 officers—a third of the force and far more than previously estimated—have dropped out of the daily lineup. Some of them may still be in houses cut off by the storm or may have simply gone off to help their families and will eventually return. But most of the missing officers have either told their superiors that they were quitting or simply walked off the job. Two officers have shot themselves to death.

Sergeant Sandoz and his urban commandos, one of the city's toughest, most elite units, have absorbed much of the violence in stride. Unlike some other officers who have succumbed to the pressure, the sergeant said he was not going anywhere except into the streets to do his job.

"You just suck it up and drive on," he said. "I'll be here as long as they need me. I'm not running away from anything."

Still, he reserved judgment, as did many others, of the officers who have abandoned the force or collapsed.

Sergeant Sandoz and his commandos have been tested by the long hours and the nagging inconveniences, like shortages of gasoline for their cars and other supplies. They expressed concerns, like many others, about the security of their jobs in a city that is taking steps to shut down for repairs. They wonder whether they will be paid for the overtime that they are logging under near-battlefield conditions.

Trying to lift spirits, the Police Department is giving every officer a five-day vacation over the next two weeks as the military steps in to replace them. Those who want to go to Las Vegas are being given plane tickets and hotel rooms for them and their families. Their breaks are beginning with physical examinations in Baton Rouge, the state capital, 75 miles north of New Orleans, inoculations against water-borne disease and other necessary medical treatment. After their breaks, the officers will start receiving psychological counseling.

Many officers said Monday that they are grateful for the breather but that they had no interest in going to Las Vegas.

"There's nothing in Las Vegas for me," said Officer Darryl Scheuermann, 41, a SWAT team member. "I'm going to see my family. I miss my wife and my dogs."

In one week, some officers have seen more violence than in a lifetime. Officer Brian French ducked sniper bullets while ferrying 50 women and children to a shelter in a commandeered rental truck.

Lt. Julie Wilson watched a fellow officer and friend being shot by looters attacking a convenience store. Lt. Billy Ceravalo and Lt. Brian Weiss lost their police station in the flooding. The floodwater also swamped a nearby hospital. Responding to a call for help, the officers raced to the hospital and began helping patients using hand operated breathing devices. They managed to keep several critically ill patients alive for hours until help arrived.

Some officers stayed in their homes as the hurricane swept over New Orleans and were forced to climb onto roofs with their families as floodwaters rose. Their pleas for help poured in over emergency radios.

"We were hearing officers on the roofs of their houses begging for someone to help them," Lieutenant Wilson said.

One officer, she said, "told me he was trapped in water up to his chest."

"I tried to get somebody out to him," she continued, but "we haven't heard from him since. I don't know if he is alive or dead."

Lieutenant Wilson's 11-year-old son, Daniel, was shipped off to neighbors. But for most of the week she had no idea where he was and worried that he feared for her as well. Now, the promise of a vacation in Las Vegas does not make her feel better.

"It's a really nice gesture," she said. "But I just want to be able to get one night's sleep without hearing helicopters. I don't think I need five days off from this, just a couple of nights."

Officer French, 25, a native of Ohio, joined the New Orleans Police Department because he wanted a chance to do "real police work."

Although he has heard city and state officials criticize the federal government as not coming fast enough, Officer French also questioned why local officers were not mustered sooner for special duty.

"They told us not to come in on Sunday, the day of the storm, to come in the next day to save money on their budget," he said.

But he never made it to work on Monday, at least not to the station house.

Officer French moved his family into a hotel. The hotel flooded, and looters attacked a nearby gasoline station. He went out into the storm, grabbed two of the looters and handcuffed them to a railing at the hotel. But, he eventually let them go.

He kept his family in the hotel for several days. But they began running out of water, and one evening shooting broke out.

For several days, Officer French rescued survivors from flooded homes. One he saved was Officer Willie Gaunt, who has since resigned.

The city's police superintendent, P. Edwin Compass III, hustled to position boats and cars before the hurricane and afterward directed rescues and charged after looters.

"We had no food," Mr. Compass told reporters on Monday. "We had no water. We ran out of ammunition. We had no vehicles. We were fighting in waist-deep water."

Mr. Compass has been accused of poorly planning for the hurricane. But he and other city officials said they were simply overwhelmed by a crisis that no municipality could handle. The disaster was compounded, they said, when federal officials in Washington ignored their cries for help for several days.

Immediately after the hurricane, he said, "we had to use so much of our manpower to fight" criminals that some rescues were delayed.

On Monday afternoon at Harrah's casino, as armored cars, fuel trucks, police cars and ambulances covered the casino's ramp and spilled into the street, Officer Russell Philibert, 38, turned to Sergeant Sandoz's unit for help. He needed a bulletproof vest. His was lost when he escaped in shorts and sneakers as water gushed into his house.

Shortly before he fled his house, he had received a radio message from another officer who lived nearby and was trapped in his attic by floodwaters in the middle of the storm. With the wind howling, he broke a window in that officer's house and dragged him to safety.

Officer Philibert said his unit had now taken shelter in a Wal-Mart. The SWAT team has moved into an elementary school on high ground, where some officers can sleep on cafeteria tables and kindergarteners' nap pads. Even the urban commandos acknowledged the strain of what they had seen.

"I might have trouble sleeping, thinking about all the horrific stuff," said Officer Robert Haar, 35. "But I'm so exhausted I just pass out."

17

Police Quitting, Overwhelmed by Chaos

Joseph B. Treaster

Reeling from the chaos of this overwhelmed city, at least 200 New Orleans police officers have walked away from their jobs and two have committed suicide, police officials said on Saturday.

Some officers told their superiors they were leaving, police officials said. Others worked for a while and then stopped showing up. Still others, for reasons not always clear, never made it in after the storm.

The absences come during a period of extraordinary stress for the New Orleans Police Department. For nearly a week, many of its 1,500 members have had to work around the clock, trying to cope with flooding, an overwhelming crush of refugees, looters and occasional snipers.

P. Edwin Compass III, the superintendent of police, said most of his officers were staying at their posts. But in an unusual note of sympathy for a top police official, he said it was understandable that many were frustrated. He said morale was "not very good."

"If I put you out on the street and made you get into gun battles all day with no place to urinate and no place to defecate, I don't think you would be too happy either," Mr. Compass said in an interview. "Our vehicles can't get any gas. The water in the street is contaminated. My officers are walking around in wet shoes."

Fire Department officials said they did not know of any firefighters who had quit. But they, too, were sympathetic to struggling emergency workers.

The New York Times, Sept 4, 2005, "Police Quitting, Overwhelmed by Chaos" by Joseph B. Treaster. © 2005 The New York Times Company. Reprinted with permission.

W.J. Riley, the assistant superintendent of police, said there were about 1,200 officers on duty on Saturday. He said the department was not sure how many officers had decided to abandon their posts and how many simply could not get to work.

Mr. Riley said some of the officers who left the force "couldn't handle the pressure" and were "certainly not the people we need in this department."

He said, "The others are not here because they lost a spouse, or their family or their home was destroyed."

Police officials did not identify the officers who took their lives, one on Saturday and the other the day before. But they said one had been a patrol officer, who a senior officer said "was absolutely outstanding." The other was an aide to Mr. Compass. The superintendent said his aide had lost his home in the hurricane and had been unable to find his family.

Because of the hurricane, many police officers and firefighters have been isolated and unable to report for duty. Others evacuated their families and have been unable to get back to New Orleans.

Still, some officers simply appear to have given up.

A Baton Rouge police officer said he had a friend on the New Orleans force who told him he threw his badge out a car window in disgust just after fleeing the city into neighboring Jefferson Parish as the hurricane approached. The Baton Rouge officer would not give his name, citing a department policy banning comments to the news media.

The officer said he had also heard of an incident in which two men in a New Orleans police cruiser were stopped in Baton Rouge on suspicion of driving a stolen squad car. The men were, in fact, New Orleans officers who had ditched their uniforms and were trying to reach a town in north Louisiana, the officer said.

"They were doing everything to get out of New Orleans," he said. "They didn't have the resources to do the job, or a plan, so they left."

The result is an even heavier burden on those who are patrolling the street, rescuing flood victims and trying to fight fires with no running water, no electricity, no reliable telephones.

Police and fire officials have been begging federal authorities for assistance and criticizing a lack of federal response for several days.

"We need help," said Charles Parent, the superintendent of the Fire Department. Mr. Parent again appealed in an interview on Saturday for replacement fire trucks and radio equipment from federal authorities. And Mr. Compass again appealed for more federal help.

"When I have officers committing suicide," Mr. Compass said, "I think we've reached a point when I don't know what more it's going to take to get the attention of those in control of the response."

The National Guard has come under criticism for not moving more quickly into New Orleans. Lt. Gen. H Steven Blum, the head of the National Guard Bureau, told reporters on Saturday that the Guard had not moved in sooner because it had not anticipated the collapse of civilian law enforcement.

Some patrol officers said morale had been low on the force even before the hurricane. One patrolman said the complaints included understaffing and a lack of equipment.

"We have to use our own shotguns," said the patrolman, who did not want to be identified by name. "This isn't theirs; this is my personal gun."

Another patrol officer said that many of the officers who had quit were younger, inexperienced officers who were overwhelmed by the task.

Some officers have expressed anger at colleagues who have stopped working. "For all you cowards that are supposed to wear the badge," one officer said on Fox News, "are you truly—can you truly wear the badge, like our motto said?"

The Police and Fire Departments are being forced to triage the calls they get for help.

The firefighters are simply not responding to some fires. In some cases, they cannot get through the flooding. But in others, they decide not to send trucks because they are needed for more serious fires.

"We can't fight every fire the way we did in the past and try to put it out," Superintendent Parent told a group of firefighters on Saturday morning at a promotion ceremony in the Algiers section of New Orleans, a dry area.

Even facing much more work than could possibly be handled, he said, it was important for him to take time out for two promotion ceremonies.

"The men need reinforcement," said Mr. Parent, who put on his last clean uniform shirt for the ceremonies elevating 22 officers to the rank of captain. "They need to see their leader and understand that the department is still here and not going to pot."

18

The Grief Police

*In Response to the Events of Sept. 11,
All Members of NYPD Must Undergo
Mental-Health Counseling, Raising Concerns
That the Tragedy Has Turned Into a Bonanza
for Overzealous Mental-Health Professionals*

Kelly Patricia O'Meara

During the Oct. 20 Madison Square Garden "Concert for New York City," a tribute to New York City's finest, Michael Moran of Ladder Company 3 stood before thousands of his peers and tens of millions of TV viewers and left no doubt as to what he thought about the deadly Sept. 11 attacks on the United States and about the man responsible. "Osama bin Laden," the hulking firefighter shouted, "you can kiss my wild Irish ass!"

The arena went wild, erupting into applause, laughter and chants of "U.S.A., U.S.A." Moran had lost his older brother and 12 other colleagues in the World Trade Center attacks and simply said publicly what a great many Americans were feeling.

Most mental-health professionals would agree that Moran, saddened and angered by his loss, was ensuring good mental health—sharing his feelings with others, getting out his anger. Given the positive reception, there seems little doubt that those in the arena and the millions watching the concert at home understood perfectly. In fact, Moran's remarks directed at the Saudi cave dweller were so well received that they were not deleted from the broadcast and are highlighted on the newly released CD of the concert.

Slightly more than a month later, however, New York City Police Commissioner Bernard Kerik, apparently concerned about how his 55,000-member force was holding up, announced mandatory mental-health counseling for every member of the New York City Police Department

(NYPD), from administrative personnel all the way up to the commissioner himself.

Although the NYPD refused numerous requests by INSIGHT for an interview about the mandatory counseling, press reports say the "mental-health" plan for the nation's largest police force isn't a new one. A similar plan was implemented following the 1995 bombing of the Alfred P. Murrah Federal Building in Oklahoma City, after which nearly 9,000 participated in some form of mental-health counseling. In fact, the Oklahoma City bombing is cited as precedent when questions are raised with the NYPD about the mandatory counseling. Again and again those asking why this is being done are told by police, political and psychiatric spokesmen to "remember all the rescue workers who committed suicide after the bombing" in Oklahoma City.

But there is little or no data about either the form of counseling provided in the aftermath of the Oklahoma City bombing or the extent to which rescue workers who allegedly committed suicide there did so before or after they had been subjected to the counseling services. There is abundant data, however, about the large amount of federal money made available for mental health after the Oklahoma City tragedy. According to the Federal Emergency Management Agency, the federal government spent almost twice as much on mental-health counseling as on relief—a whopping $4.1 million, compared with just $1.7 million for housing assistance and $468,000 for replacing personal property.

While the level of care provided by mental-health professionals after the Oklahoma City attack seems impressive, INSIGHT has learned from survivors of the bombing that attending counseling sessions was made a requisite to qualifying for financial assistance. According to one survivor who asked not to be identified, the authorities were careful not to "say we had to go to counseling, but we didn't get any financial assistance until we did. They just kept suggesting that we go every time we sat down to talk about the various benefits." She tells INSIGHT that after her first counseling session she was put on two different mind-altering drugs. Critics of the mental-health profession's growing reliance on psychotropic remedies tell INSIGHT they fear this may be in store for New York City's finest. Advocates say they see it as a check against crazed officers running amok.

The driving force behind the call for mandatory counseling is concern that the tragic events of Sept. 11 may linger well beyond mood depression, a normal human response to horrific events, and turn into a mental illness such as posttraumatic stress disorder (PTSD), which may show itself months or even years after the event.

The subjective criteria for PTSD is defined by the American Psychiatric Association's *Diagnostic and Statistical Manual of Mental Disorders* as: "1) the person experienced, witnessed or was confronted with an event or events that involved actual or threatened death or serious injury, or a threat to the physical integrity of self or others, and 2) the person's response involved intense fear, helplessness or horror." By that definition, it could be said, all Americans who watched or saw even video footage of the attacks on the World Trade Center or the Pentagon could be "victims" of this so-called mental illness.

Under cover of getting help to those in the NYPD who may suffer break-downs, a three-step approach has been taken to evaluate the entire force. The first is a kind of group-therapy session to encourage members of the force to discuss the events of Sept. 11 and learn about mental-health programs available to them. Step two is access to an "anonymous hot line" so those who want additional counseling can be given "confidential" appointments. And step three is a "mental-health fair" for members of the NYPD and their families who may want to discuss the events of Sept. 11.

All the mental-health professionals running this program are "volunteers" from Columbia University who will bill the New York City Police Foundation, a nonprofit organization providing $10 million for this mental-health counseling. Columbia is to keep no records on the officers who seek counseling beyond the introductory session.

Critics of this mandatory mental-health counseling tell INSIGHT they wonder whether forcing such counseling may, in fact, be harmful. Elliot Valenstein, professor emeritus of psychology at the University of Michigan, says: "I'm quite skeptical of any plan that would require mandatory counseling for all 55,000 New York City police officers. I have no doubt that there are some police officers who are emotionally unstable, overly aggressive, prejudiced, under too much stress and so forth, and some of them might benefit from counseling. But if a massive mandatory counseling program is undertaken, I view it as highly unlikely that it would attract the caliber of competent counselors who would be able to help those who need help."

Valenstein continues: "I recognize that there may be problems dealing with the events of Sept. 11, but I think mandatory counseling is not the solution. There is the possibility that a mandatory counseling program would lead to a lot of perfunctory prescriptions of medication that would not be followed up adequately for adverse side effects. For example, SSRIs [selective serotonin reuptake inhibitors] tend to make some people more impulsive. This may be a good thing for depressed people, but there are obvious dangers of making people carrying weapons impulsive, and there are many other side effects of these drugs."

If NYPD officers are prescribed antidepressants, must they take them? Bill Genet, a spokesman for the Patrolmen's Benevolent Association, tells INSIGHT, "It's a very involved process, but the department's policy is that they'll decide individual cases."

On the other hand, if the mandatory counseling really is anonymous, as the program has been described, how will the department know which of its officers are taking or have refused to take mind-altering drugs? While Genet makes it clear that he was not speaking for the NYPD, he says he understands and supports the decision for counseling. "This is" he says, "about anybody dealing with a traumatic event having a reaction. Trauma is a shock, and it's a shock to all the body's systems. The thing with these emergency workers is that they shut down the bodily shock because they have to get their job done, and that's why it's called post-traumatic stress. This accumulates, and there comes a time at which it all shuts down and stops."

Tana Dineen, a licensed psychologist and author of *Manufacturing Victims: What the Psychology Industry Is Doing to People*, tells INSIGHT, "I don't know why the NYPD is doing this. Other than appearing to be a civil-rights violation, it sounds like an introductory advertising session to lure in potential client/patients. The police will be told they're suffering from mental illness, and they'll be encouraged to come forward and get the help they need. There are absolutely no data to support the idea that talking about tragic events helps, but there are data that show some people are harmed by talking about it. The idea will get presented, however, that if their feelings go untreated for too long they might need help or may be developing PTSD or some other mental illness. Counselors will tell them that they can help but, in reality, people can end up ruminating more about the negative things, worrying if they have some psychological illness, and become more debilitated."

Dineen says she tends "to look at psychology as a business that needs clients and patients. The going formula is 'trauma equals victims equals patients equals profits.' These [NYPD] guys are going into a promotional session, which will lure them into the idea that they're victims, turn them into patients and create profits for the psychiatric industry. That's one of the problems with my profession—we have all the pat answers. I say don't trust the experts."

According to Dineen, "What you hear from my profession is what might go wrong if people don't get their help. We live in a therapeutic society, and we're told that everything can be fixed or cured. One of the costs to our society is that people have lost the breath of human experience—we've been convinced that we're not supposed to feel bad things. All of these feelings these people have are natural and necessary, not mental illness. I think my profession is selling some pretty dangerous answers, and people need to be warned about the dangers of some of the theories and bogus therapies that are being sold."

Ira Warheit, a Manhattan periodontist, can attest to the abuses that can occur when overzealous psychiatrists want to "help." Warheit spent three days volunteering at ground zero wherever he was needed—giving medical advice, passing out food and working on the bucket brigade. While taking a rest break at one of the staging centers around ground zero, he was confronted by a psychiatrist, Antonio Abad. They began talking, but within minutes the psychiatrist excused himself. He returned with a NYPD officer to have Warheit removed to Bellevue Hospital. "I tried to explain," Warheit says, "that there was nothing wrong with me, that I was a doctor volunteering, but the cop physically restrained me and I was transported to the psychiatric hospital." Once at Bellevue, Warheit continues, "a female doctor comes up to me and says she has some questions. I told her I'd be happy to answer her questions, but I wasn't going into the hospital. So she calls over two goons and they forcibly put me in restraints and shoot me full of Haldol."

This drugging of Warheit went on for days until he was required by law to be taken before a judge to decide if he was to be committed to the hospital. Within minutes of hearing Warheit's story, the judge released him. The respected doctor now is suing the state for wrongfully seizing and incarcerating him at Bellevue. According to Stuart Shaw, Warheit's attorney, "A claim has been filed for Ira for false arrest and false imprisonment. There is a great deal of investigating that has to be done, but it seems strange to me that a man like this would be physically restrained and injured. He committed no crime, was not trespassing and in fact was volunteering his services. It just seems to me that before a reasonable man can put another man in a straitjacket you have to really see something strange, and it just isn't so in this case."

Shaw continues: "What I'm afraid of is that Ira's case is just the tip of the iceberg. I'm afraid there may be a lot of little people—police and firemen and others that also were put in Bellevue by this guy and others like him. It could be years before we know how many were sent there, and it will be difficult to get the data because many won't want to talk about what happened, and the hospital will claim privacy rights. I've handled a lot of commitments but none of the stature of Ira. His civil rights have been violated, and my intention is to sue in federal court."

Ayal Lindeman, a volunteer emergency medical technician from Rockland County, N.Y., already had witnessed the seizure of another volunteer at ground zero when he met Warheit and learned his story. Lindeman tells INSIGHT, "There's this doctor who was being told that he's going to the hospital, and he's saying 'I don't want to go,' and this psychiatrist gets the cops and they handcuff the poor guy and off he goes to Bellevue. This is a doctor who has been volunteering at ground zero—and this psychiatrist, Abad, is having him committed and pumped full of Haldol. It was just insanity what was happening. I was livid."

Lindeman recalls how the emergency workers felt about the presence of so many psychiatrists at ground zero. "I was sitting with these firemen and police who were on break," he says, "and this woman walks up and is handing out pamphlets for counseling services. One of the police officers stood up and told her 'Hey, we don't need you giving us these things,' and he pulled out a handful of cards he said he had been given in just a 12-hour period. These guys were glaring at this woman. They all heard about the incarceration incidents with Warheit, and another guy pipes up and says, 'If he pulls that crap with me I'll cap his ass.'"

Lindeman concludes in his heavy New York accent, "The thing is, these guys did great, they did their job. I'm sure the commissioner is doing this mandatory counseling because he loves his guys and is trying to help them. But don't do anything to harm them; don't force them into anything they don't want. Sure, there are some guys who are really hurting, but they don't have mental illnesses. They aren't crazy."

19

PTSD Rate Tripled Among N.Y. Police Officers

Barbara Boughton

LOS ANGELES—A new study shows that the rate of posttraumatic stress disorder among New York City policemen and women more than tripled after Sept. 11, 2001, Dr. Charles Marmar said at a meeting on posttraumatic stress disorder sponsored by the Foundation for Psychocultural Research.

In a study of 337 police officers—242 of whom worked in New York— Dr. Marmar and his colleagues found that the rate of PTSD increased from 7% to 24% among New York City police officers after Sept. 11, while in the San Francisco area, which was also studied, the rate stayed the same.

"The study shows the impact of catastrophic events on first responders, which is important in our civil defense. If we can't protect the health of first responders, then we are all in jeopardy in an age of terrorism," Dr. Marmar said just a few weeks before the nation was placed under a heightened security.

The study, in which data are still being collected, began with 747 police officers in New York and the San Francisco area. The officers were tested for PTSD symptoms and interviewed for information about their exposure to traumas such as shoot-outs and car accidents. At baseline, the New York City police officers had a slightly higher number of PTSD symptoms than officers

Clinical Psychiatry News, March 2003 v31 i3 p32(1) "PTSD Rate Tripled Among N.Y. Police Officers" by Barbara Boughton. © 2003 International Medical News Group. Reprinted with permission.

in the Bay area, said Dr. Marmar at the meeting, also sponsored by the University of California, Los Angeles.

The quality of the police officers' social support and work environment also affected the development of PTSD, according to Dr. Marmar. "Experiencing negative life events in the year after 9/11 was important in the development of PTSD," he added.

The strongest predictors of which officers would develop PTSD after Sept. 11 were their level of panic at the time of the event and the extent to which they disassociated from the tragedy. The amount of exposure the policemen and women had to the Sept. 11 terrorist attack also had high predictive power of PTSD, said Dr. Marmar, of the University of California, San Francisco. "The more terrified they were and the longer they were terrified, the more likely they were to have PTSD symptoms later," he said.

Not surprisingly the New York police officers had poorer quality of life overall than did the San Francisco area officers. There was a sharp increase, for instance, in reports of impaired sleep after Sept. 11 among the New York City police officers.

There were no significant differences in the demographics of the two groups, no difference in baseline critical incidence exposure or routine work stress. And there were no differences in baseline symptoms of stress when the two groups were compared, Dr. Marmar said.

The police officers studied in Dr. Marmar's research were 20% women, half white, and half from minority groups. At baseline and before Sept. 11, being Hispanic was a predictor of having PTSD. Other predictors of PTSD at baseline were poor social support and routine work stress, such as a hostile environment for minorities. "Routine work stress was very important and was more predictive of developing PTSD than total cumulative exposure to an incident such as a shoot-out," Dr. Marmar said.

Before Sept. 11, the degree of the officers' peritraumatic disassociation as well as peritraumatic terror at the time of a crisis, such as a shoot-out, predicted PTSD.

Even before Sept. 11, almost half of the officers complained of sleep difficulties. Lack of a social support network and a poor work environment were the strongest predictors of sleep problems, Dr. Marmar said. "This is a real problem, because these officers are in a profession when rapid judgments are often needed," he added.

V

DISASTER RESPONSE: CRITICISM AND RECOMMENDATIONS

Past disasters and other national problems have tested response strategies by various governmental agencies. The involvement of many different organizations and the magnitude of the crises have made it difficult to coordinate and focus rescue and law enforcement efforts in the most effective way. Many times, the outcome was a disappointment to victims as well as police or rescue. The most recent catastrophic events of 9/11 and Hurricane Katrina have focused public attention on improving crisis responses.

20

Mayor's Plan Puts Police Commissioner in Charge of Disaster Control

Thomas J. Lueck

Mayor Michael R. Bloomberg announced the first major proposal of his re-election campaign yesterday, saying that he would seek authority for New York City's police commissioner to take command during terrorist attacks or other disasters at major bridges, tunnels, airports and other transportation hubs.

Mr. Bloomberg said the change could better coordinate the response to a large-scale emergency involving several jurisdictions. Because the commissioner would be commanding officers of the Metropolitan Transportation Authority and the Port Authority of New York and New Jersey, the proposal would require the approval of both governors.

The mayor, who was joined by Thomas H. Kean, a former New Jersey governor and co-chairman of the Sept. 11 commission, described his plan as part of a broader set of proposals for public safety that include sending text messages to people's cellphones in emergencies and opening a Manhattan gun court for weapons offenders.

His proposals come less than six weeks before the Nov. 8 election, and were offered yesterday in what Mr. Bloomberg said would be a "series of policy addresses" outlining his vision for a second term.

The New York Times, Sept 30, 2005, "Mayor's Plan Puts Police Commissioner in Charge of Disaster Control" by Thomas J. Lueck. © 2005 The New York Times Company. Reprinted with permission.

"The ideas I propose will be ambitious, but also achievable and afford-able," he said. "Unlike my opponent, I will not make any proposals that would require raising taxes."

Mr. Ferrer, asked about the mayor's proposals, said the city would be bet-ter served by working through its existing Office of Emergency Management to "coordinate all responders in the city." His prepared statement chided the mayor's plan as overdue and overly dramatic.

"It took Mike Bloomberg four years to come up with a plan that reads like last week's episode of 'C.S.I.,'" the statement said, referring to a television crime drama.

In appearing with Mr. Kean, the mayor sought to portray his plan as a log-ical outgrowth of breakdowns in command, logistics and communication that hampered initial responses to the Sept. 11 attack in New York and to Hurri-cane Katrina.

Mr. Bloomberg and Mr. Kean both said the plan was meant to create the kind of "unity of command" in the New York region that was called for by the report prepared last year by the Sept. 11 commission. Under the proposal, the states, the M.T.A., the Port Authority and the police would agree in ad-vance about what constituted a serious enough emergency for the New York commissioner to take charge.

The proposal would create an additional seat on the board of the Metro-politan Transportation Authority and on the board of the Port Authority, both to be assigned to a representative of the city police commissioner. Such a pro-posal would expand the already broad powers of Commissioner Raymond W. Kelly, whose police force was recently given wider control over emergencies involving hazardous substances.

"In an emergency, you have to have one agency in charge, and the logical one—because of its size and sophistication—is the N.Y.P.D.," Mr. Bloomberg said. Jordan Barowitz, a spokesman for the mayor's campaign, said the plan would involve joint training for the Port Authority Police Department, which has 1,600 officers, the M.T.A. police, with 1,500 officers, and the New York City Police Department, with 36,000 officers.

Although informed of the proposal in advance, neither Gov. George E. Pataki of New York nor Acting Gov. Richard J. Codey of New Jersey has signed off on it, Mr. Bloomberg said. The approval of the two governors, or their successors, would be critical: The New York governor has traditionally exercised firm control over the M.T.A., and the governors of the two states jointly control the Port Authority.

Through their aides, Mr. Pataki and Mr. Codey responded cordially yes-terday, saying they would review the mayor's proposal, as did a spokesman for the Port Authority.

But the plan seemed certain to encounter hurdles, including objections from police unions and the deeply entrenched rivalries over control of the two large transportation agencies.

Thomas J. Kelly, a spokesman for the M.T.A., suggested yesterday that the mayor designate one of four representatives he already appoints to the 17-member board as a representative of the commissioner, instead of adding a seat.

Mr. Kelly said the mayor's proposal might create confusion and resentment over the law enforcement chain of command. "This a very delicate issue," he said. "You can't negotiate these protocols in a press release."

Gus Danese, the president of the Port Authority Policemen's Benevolent Association, whose members patrol the region's three international airports and other hubs, said he opposed the plan. "What does Kelly know about Kennedy Airport?" he said. "We have 300 officers working there every day, and they are the ones with the experience."

21

9/11 Exposed Deadly Flaws in Rescue Plan

Jim Dwyer, Kevin Flynn, and Ford Fessenden

Minutes after the south tower collapsed at the World Trade Center, police helicopters hovered near the remaining tower to check its condition. "About 15 floors down from the top, it looks like it's glowing red," the pilot of one helicopter, Aviation 14, radioed at 10:07 a.m. "It's inevitable."

Seconds later, another pilot reported: "I don't think this has too much longer to go. I would evacuate all people within the area of that second building."

Those clear warnings, captured on police radio tapes, were transmitted 21 minutes before the building fell, and officials say they were relayed to police officers, most of whom managed to escape. Yet most firefighters never heard those warnings, or earlier orders to get out. Their radio system failed frequently that morning. Even if the radio network had been reliable, it was not linked to the police system. And the police and fire commanders guiding the rescue efforts did not talk to one another during the crisis.

Cut off from critical information, at least 121 firefighters, most in striking distance of safety, died when the north tower fell, an analysis by *The New York Times* has found.

Faced with devastating attacks, the city's emergency personnel formed an indelible canvas of sacrifice, man by man and woman by woman. They helped rescue thousands. They saved lives. They risked their own.

From the first moments to the last, however, their efforts were plagued by failures of communication, command and control.

Now, after months of grief, both the Fire and Police Departments are approaching the end of delicate internal reviews of their responses to the attack. Those reviews have concluded that major changes are needed in how the agencies go about their work and prepare for the next disaster, senior officials say.

A six-month examination by *The Times* found that the rescuers' ability to save themselves and others was hobbled by technical difficulties, a history of tribal feuding and management lapses that have been part of the emergency response culture in New York City and other regions for years.

- When the firefighters needed to communicate, their radio system failed, just as it had in those same buildings eight years earlier, during the response to the 1993 bombing at the trade center. No other agency lost communications on Sept. 11 as broadly, or to such devastating effect, as the Fire Department.

- Throughout the crisis, the two largest emergency departments, Police and Fire, barely spoke to coordinate strategy or to share intelligence about building conditions.

- During those final minutes, most firefighters inside the north tower did not know the other building had crumbled, and how urgent it was for them to get out. Instead, dozens of firefighters were catching their breath on the 19th floor of the tower, witnesses say. Others were awaiting orders in the lobby. Still others were evacuating the disabled and the frightened.

- To this day, the Fire Department cannot say just how many firefighters were sent into the towers, and where they died. It lost track of them, in part because some companies did not check in with chiefs. Individual firefighters jumped on overcrowded trucks, against policy. Others, ordered off the fire trucks, grabbed rides in cars.

- The city's intricate network of safety coverage showed signs of unraveling that morning because of the headlong rush to Lower Manhattan. Police officers left their posts, senior police officials said. A chief with the Emergency Medical Service said they had no ambulances for more than 400 calls. The region's bridges, tunnels, and ports were drained of protection, said the chief of the Port Authority police.

- Although Mayor Rudolph W. Giuliani created the Office of Emergency Management in 1996 and spent nearly $25 million to coordinate emergency response, trade center officials said the agency had not conducted an emergency exercise there that included the Fire Department, the police and the Port Authority's emergency staff.

The Fire Department began its first self-examination in December, when nearly 50 senior fire officials took part in a two-day planning exercise with the United States Naval War College. The college evaluators concluded: "As a function of command and control, it was evident that the Fire Department has no formal system to evaluate problems or develop plans for multiple

complex events. It was equally evident that the Fire Department has conducted very little formal planning at the operational level."

Thomas Von Essen, the city's fire commissioner from 1996 through 2001,
and a former president of the main fire union, said he agreed with that analysis, which was undertaken to explore the ability to respond to major disasters.
The fire commissioner has limited authority to hold senior chiefs accountable,
Mr. Von Essen said, because nearly all enjoy Civil Service protection.

"The pain is still there and it'll be there forever," Mr. Von Essen said. "But
you have to start thinking about the reality of the world that we live in today.
And that demands better leadership, more accountable leadership, a better-
trained leadership, a more disciplined leadership that then filters down to a
better-trained and more disciplined set of troops."

Many chiefs, for their part, have long cited Mr. Von Essen's leadership as a
major department failing. The results of other reviews, covering police and
fire performance, are due within a few weeks from the consulting firm
McKinsey & Company.

For Mr. Von Essen, a searing topic is the high number of firefighter casu-
alties in the north tower. The collapse of the south tower after 57 minutes
shocked the fire commanders. Yet more than a third of the 343 firefighter
deaths were in the north tower, even though it stood 29 minutes longer. The
failure of more firefighters to escape in those 29 minutes baffles Mr. Von Essen.
He believes many got word to leave.

"Should we know the answers to all of that stuff by now? Absolutely,"
Mr. Von Essen said. "But do we really want to know the answers to these
questions? I don't think the department really wants to know."

He could not explain why the police had not reported to fire commanders, the official leaders of the response. "That day the police did not hook up
with the Fire Department," Mr. Von Essen said. "I don't know why."

Too many firefighters, he said, were sent into the towers, and too many
came without being told they were needed. "I've been a firefighter since 1970,
and have often stood on floors where we needed 10 people and had 30,"
Mr. Von Essen said. "There's a lack of control that's dangerous on an everyday
basis to firefighters."

Police Commissioner Raymond W. Kelly said the eagerness to respond
could put both police officers and the city at risk. "People got on the subway
and came down," he said. "We need a much more controlled response these
days. Why? Because we have to be concerned about secondary events."

Both Mr. Von Essen and Mr. Kelly said rigorous scrutiny of their agencies
was vital. "We should not second-guess the people at the scene, or the way
they handled it that day—they did a terrific job at the scene, and you will not
find better chiefs anywhere in the country than the ones who ran things,"
Mr. Von Essen said. "I think we should second-guess our procedures, our
policies, our history."

Mr. Kelly, who led the police a decade ago and returned in January, said:
"Now, literally, that the dust has settled, we are obligated to look at these

things and to learn lessons. We are in the business of emergency response. That's our business, every day. We have to think in a systematic way."

To explore the emergency response on Sept. 11, *Times* reporters interviewed more than 100 firefighters, police officers, emergency medical workers, government officials and witnesses. Those interviews were supplemented by reviews of 1,000 pages of oral histories collected by the Fire Department, 20 hours of police and fire radio transmissions and 4,000 pages of city records, and by creating a database that tracked 2,500 eyewitness reports of sightings of fire companies, individual firefighters and other rescue personnel that morning. The city has refused to release thousands of pages of accounts by firefighters and their superiors.

On Friday, Fire Commissioner Nicholas Scoppetta said the city intended to create a radio channel that could be shared by police officers and firefighters, among other changes. "There is no question there were communications problems at this catastrophic incident," he said.

Bernard B. Kerik, the police commissioner at the time, said he did not believe that any communication problems between the agencies had significantly affected their performance. "I was not made aware that day that we were having any difficulty coordinating," he said.

COMMUNICATIONS

"DOWN TO THE LOBBY," BUT NO ONE CAME

Battalion Chief Joseph Pfeifer held his two-way radio to his ear. He tried to edge away from the noise in the north tower lobby, hoping the reception would improve. Still no good. Minutes before, he stood on a street corner in Lower Manhattan and watched as American Airlines Flight 11 flew directly overhead and crashed into the north tower of the World Trade Center.

Now, as the first chief to reach the building, he was sending fire companies up the stairs, including one led by his own brother, Lt. Kevin Pfeifer, who did not survive. Then he found that he had no way to speak with the rescuers starting the long climb: once again, the firefighters were having terrible radio problems inside this high-rise building.

More than eight years earlier, hundreds of firefighters came to the World Trade Center after terrorists tried to bomb one of the towers off its foundation. "Communications were a serious problem from the outset," Anthony L. Fusco, then chief of the department, had warned in a 1994 federal report on the Fire Department's response to that attack. They had lost touch with firefighters trying to extinguish the smoldering bomb crater underground, and with others who had climbed clear to the top of the towers.

Now, Chief Pfeifer tried to turn on a device known as a repeater, which had been installed at 5 World Trade Center to help solve those problems by boosting the radio signal strength. The repeater didn't seem to be working, Chief Pfeifer said later.

Another fire chief arriving at the trade center tried a second repeater in his department car. That did not work, either.

As hundreds of firefighters climbed toward the upper floors where 1,100 people were trapped, one communications post after another was proving unreliable. Even commanders spread among four separate posts could not get through.

"I wasn't getting communications and I couldn't communicate into the building," Deputy Assistant Chief Albert J. Turi, now retired, said in an interview.

By 9:30 a.m., after both planes had struck, a rumor was circulating that a third hijacked plane was headed to New York. Assistant Chief Joseph Callan recalled feeling the north tower move. "I made the decision that the building was no longer safe," the chief told the Fire Department's oral history interviewers.

"All units in Building 1," he announced over the radio at 9:32. "All units in Building 1, come out, down to the lobby. Everybody down to the lobby."

Virtually no one answered his call. It seemed that few people, apart from those standing near him, heard it. Chief Peter Hayden, who was at the scene, said: "We had ordered the firefighters down, but we weren't getting acknowledgments. We were very concerned about it."

When Assistant Chief Donald J. Burns arrived, he reminded his colleagues of the severe communication problems during the 1993 bombing, Chief Hayden recalled. Commanders were forced that day to rely on runners to deliver vital messages. "Pre-plan and build contingency plans," Chief Burns wrote in the 1994 federal report. "Our effectiveness is only as good as our ability to communicate." On Sept. 11, he took command of operations in the south tower, the second building to be hit, and was killed.

The radios the firefighters carried into the buildings that day were identical to the ones they had brought into the trade center eight years earlier. By the department's own estimation, those radios, some of which were 15 years old, were outdated. "There were problems with the radios at virtually every high-rise fire," said Deputy Chief Nicholas J. Visconti, who was the commander in Midtown Manhattan for three years.

The radio problems, many officials say, are a symptom of the department's resistance to new technology. "We're dinosaurs," said Richard J. Sheirer, the former director of the city's Office of Emergency Management and a former fire dispatcher. David Rosensweig, the president of the fire alarm dispatchers' union, says the city has been talking for more than a decade about improving its computer-aided dispatch system.

Early in 2001, the department replaced its old analog radios with a new generation that used digital technology. The new models operated on higher frequencies and were judged somewhat better at penetrating buildings, but several firefighters said they had been unable to communicate in emergencies, so the digital radios were pulled from service in March 2001.

Other cities have been no swifter at solving the problems of communication at high-rise fires, industry professionals said.

The department did try to make some improvements after the terrorist bombing at the trade center in 1993, like the repeater installed on 5 World Trade Center to amplify the radio signal. The city police and Port Authority police have similar repeaters and neither agency experienced significant radio problems on Sept. 11, officials said.

Even now, the source of the Fire Department's radio problems remains murky. "I've asked five people in the Fire Department already, and I get a different answer from most of them," Mr. Von Essen said.

For a while, officials from the Fire Department and the Port Authority said the Fire Department repeater had been disabled by debris from the first plane. Now, however, Port Authority officials say they have proof that the repeater did work: tape recordings discovered in January or February with fire radio transmissions that were successfully routed through the repeater that day.

Some companies on higher floors were able to communicate. Squad 252 had been leaving the north tower, but it decided to help another company, Rescue 1, that was on a higher floor, said Firefighter Steve Modica, who heard the two companies talk over the radio. Neither company survived.

Other firefighters appear to have been using one radio channel while evacuation orders went out over another, according to the accounts of several firefighters.

In many other instances, firefighters said they simply never got the order to leave because the radio system worked only intermittently. Firefighter Modica said he tried different channels, without success, to reach a friend who had gone up ahead of him.

"It's a disgrace," he said. "The police are talking to each other. It's a nobrainer: Get us what they're using. We send people to the moon, and you mean to tell me a firefighter can't talk to a guy two floors above him?"

COMMAND

DISTRUST SEPARATES POLICE AND FIRE

Almost an hour after the first plane struck, the wind shifted, and for a moment the blanket of smoke on the roofs of the towers lifted slightly. Perhaps there was a chance to save some people at the top of the buildings.

"As soon as it's feasible, we need to go on the roof," one police officer said on his radio.

From the air, a second police officer replied: "Aviation 12, we're taking a look; we're going to look at the northwest corner of north building." On the ground, a team of police emergency service officers gathered rappelling outfits for the helicopters.

For fire chiefs, the police helicopters could also be invaluable: the firefighters' climb to the 80th floor during the 1993 attack lasted four hours, and the blaze in the north tower was 15 floors above that. Even if roof rescues proved too risky, as police commanders later decided, the fire chiefs wanted to see what the fires were doing to the buildings.

"At one point, I was asked to get the operations with the helicopter into motion," Chief Pfeifer said in his oral history, but he could not reach the dispatcher.

He recited problems—a missing radio, jammed phone lines, no one answering—but the simplest solution of all was not available to Chief Pfeifer: a face-to-face conversation with a police supervisor. No police supervisors reported to the lobby command posts set up by the Fire Department to coordinate efforts. The police established their command post three blocks away at the corner of Church and Vesey Streets.

In the end, no firefighter boarded the helicopters. When police pilots reported "large pieces" falling from the south tower 10 minutes before it collapsed, only police officers had seen it from the sky, and only police officers on the ground could hear their warnings. When the pilots saw that the north building was near collapse 21 minutes before it fell, their warnings reached some police officers on the street and inside the tower, but not firefighters. Although the two departments had talked for years about establishing a common radio channel, they could not reach agreement.

Nearly every state, including New York, and the federal government have adopted a structure for managing crises known as the incident command system, in which agencies agree in advance who will be in charge. New York City has not. The Police and Fire Departments did not work together that day, and they rarely did before.

Allen H. Hoehl, a retired police commander, disputed the idea that officers routinely refuse to work with fire officials. He said he had often designated a ranking officer to serve as a liaison.

Other police officials maintain that sharing command with the Fire Department is difficult because firefighters lack paramilitary discipline.

Lt. John McArdle, a member of the police Emergency Service Unit, was blunt in his views of the firefighters. "If someone tells them to do something, they say, 'I don't work for him,'" he said in an interview. "If a police sergeant tells a group of cops to hold up, they do."

Senior fire chiefs spelled out their resentment of the police during the Naval War College evaluation in December. Asked about interagency cooperation, some in the senior fire staff wrote: "There is none"; "You will never change the P.D."; "Let them put snowplows on the front end of their cars. They want to do everything else"; "There's a reason people hate cops"; "Most agencies try to be cooperative, helpful, but the police have a very limited ability to cooperate."

After years of bickering, the two agencies did not squabble on Sept. 11. They simply did not communicate. "There was not a link," Police Commissioner Kelly acknowledged.

Asked if the incident command system called for police, fire and other agencies to share a post, Commissioner Kelly said: "Well, it should. And we're getting there."

On paper, the Police and Fire Department have agreed since 1993 to share the police helicopters during high-rise fires, and to practice together. Neither agency has any records of joint drills, but Sgt. Mike Wysokowski, a police spokesman, said that members of the police Aviation Unit believed a "familiarization flight" was conducted for the Fire Department a year, or perhaps a year and half, before Sept. 11.

No familiarization flights were taken from Sept. 11 through mid-June, he said.

As important as helicopter access might have been on Sept. 11, the gulf between the two departments is formed around everyday, earthbound business.

On that morning, the Police Department's elite Emergency Service Unit sent teams into both towers. Trained in rescue tactics, the E.S.U. police officers often tackle the same kinds of work as firefighters.

In the stairwells, members of both services helped each other carry equipment, administer first aid and pass messages.

The police emergency officers did not, however, check in with the fire commanders who were in charge of the rescue.

"They report to nobody and they go and do whatever they want," said Chief Turi, who retired earlier this year as a senior safety officer for the Fire Department.

CONTROL

DISCIPLINE BROKE DOWN IN EAGERNESS TO HELP

News of the trade center attacks broke as shifts changed at firehouses across the city. At Ladder Company 16 on East 67th Street, four firefighters who were scheduled to go off duty wanted to stay and help. But Lt. Dan Williams told them "to get the hell off the rig," he said later. "Why? I took one look at the TV and I said, 'We're going to lose people here today.' There was no doubt in my mind.

"A person can control a certain amount of people," he said. "I was in the military, the Marine Corps, for four years, in Vietnam. So I was thinking that way. I'm not putting anyone else down there. We're going to be in enough danger without putting more people in a situation like that. I didn't say it nicely. I said, 'Get off the rig.'"

The men got off. Then they went outside and caught rides to the trade center in a police car and a city bus. One was killed in the collapse of the north tower.

He was among the 60 off-duty firefighters to die. Some came from second jobs, one from a golf course. Many bypassed staging areas and commanders with whom they were supposed to check in, fire officials said. Several on-duty companies led by veteran officers did the same.

Those who responded so impulsively were upholding the Fire Department's finest tradition: the selfless struggle to save the endangered. But they were also rushing to fight a fire that department officials had already decided was unfightable. And they did so in such numbers, with so little coordination, that some fire officials are now questioning whether the department known as the Bravest acted too bravely that day.

"Courage is not enough," Mr. Von Essen said. "The fact that the guys are so dedicated comes back to hurt them down the line."

Many officials now say the city needs a more measured and disciplined response, which would allow officials to hold back resources in case of a second incident. "You have to train them," said the Port Authority police chief, Joseph Morris. "You can't have everybody coming in."

Port Authority police officers also flocked to the scene, leaving posts at bridges and tunnels, Chief Morris said. Ambulance crews converged on Lower Manhattan, leaving much of the city sparsely covered. At one point, the city's Emergency Medical Service had no ambulances for some 400 backed-up emergency calls, its senior officer on duty, Walter Kowalczyk, said later. Fire officials said that just after the collapses, more than 100 ambulances, nearly one-third of the fleet on duty, went to the buildings.

"As we've said at so many funerals, cops and firemen run in when everybody else runs out," said Commissioner Kelly, adding, "So when you say, 'Hey, we don't want you to go,' it is really contrary to the reason why you signed on for this kind of work."

The Naval War College analysts found that the lack of planning left the Fire Department vulnerable to losing control at a major disaster. "It was clear," the college's report said, "that the responses above the tactical level are largely handled 'on the fly,' with tremendous gaps in command and control."

The loss of control was not evident in the demeanor of commanders on Sept. 11; videotapes show them responding calmly to crises. Later, though, some firefighters spoke of an aimlessness to the efforts. "Nobody had a plan," said Firefighter Modica, an aide to a chief lost in the north tower.

When Jay Swithers, a captain and paramedic assigned to the Fire Department's Bureau of Health Services, arrived at a triage center operated by the Emergency Medical Service, he could not find Fire Chief Raymond M. Downey, who led the Special Operations Command and whom Captain Swithers would be working with.

"Nobody could tell me where he was," Captain Swithers said in an oral history. "Most of the E.M.S. people didn't know what special command was or who Chief Downey was." The chief died in the collapse.

Certainly, the attacks exceeded anything emergency planners had anticipated. In the West, some fire departments have coordinated massive responses to brush fires. But in New York, mock disaster drills rarely draw more than 100 firefighters. On Sept. 11, the department used nearly 1,000.

"On that day, Sept. 11, all the plans, all the scenarios that we had developed, everything, everything was blown up," James Ellson, a former deputy in the city's Office of Emergency Management, said recently.

Senior fire officials said that even as they drove to the towers they knew the fire was too large to fight. "It was evident that we weren't going to be able to get to people above the fire," Thomas Fitzpatrick, a deputy commissioner, said in his oral history.

In the confusion, though, firefighters continued to charge up the stairs with lengths of hose that weighed 38 pounds. Some suffered chest pains. Others could not tell one building from the other. Such confusion occurred so often that Chief Pfeifer had "Tower 1" written in marker on the command post in the north tower lobby. And no one in authority ever realized that a stairwell was open in the south tower. At least 18 people ultimately escaped from above the impact zone that way, but word of their route never reached hundreds of others trapped above.

Over all, however, nearly everyone below the floors where the planes struck escaped, helped by rescuers. Sharon Premoli, an executive vice president with Beast Financial Systems, said she was comforted by the sight of the ascending firefighters.

"I felt better, I felt safe," she said. "They were the reason."

Lt. Brian Becker, who escaped from the north tower with his unit, Engine Company 28, said it was simplistic to view the day in terms of heroism or blame.

"It was a series of random events that killed thousands and saved hundreds," he said. "Not many people did anything right that day, but not many people did anything wrong that day either."

Even today, fire officials cannot say where many firefighters died, in part because the magnetic command boards, which the department used to track companies, were lost in the collapses. The Times tried to track those locations using a database that compiled more than 2,500 sightings of fire companies and individuals.

Based on those eyewitnesses, The Times concluded that 33 fire companies, which lost 121 men, were operating in the north tower when it collapsed. Of the other firefighters who died, the eyewitness accounts placed 97 in the south tower, 34 in the Marriott Hotel and 13 outside the building.

The locations of 78 firefighters could not be traced. Fire Department records indicate that many of them had been assigned to the south tower.

SACRIFICE

"WE'LL COME DOWN IN A FEW MINUTES"

Above the impact zone, 800 people were trapped. Below it, the dying north tower was emptying. After more than an hour of evacuation, the stream of civilians was a trickle.

Then the south tower fell, and people watched around the world.

Not across the plaza. There, the crash registered only as a shudder in the bones of people up and down the north tower. "Everybody felt it and they didn't know exactly what it was," Firefighter Frank Campagna said in an oral history interview.

"The building was still standing," he said. "So we just kept going up the stairs."

On the 51st floor, three court officers felt the violent lurch and decided to get out. "We did not know that the south tower collapsed—never mind that the north tower was going to go," said Deputy Chief Joseph Baccellieri, who had rushed into the tower along with two other court officers, Sgts. Alfred Moscola and Andrew Wender. The three started down.

By that time, firefighters had been climbing stairs for more than an hour. Their mission seemed unclear. After the collapse, Chief Pfeifer radioed an order to get out. That message and others reached chiefs on some floors, but not on others. No firefighters appeared to have the hard information the police got. None seemed to know that the other building had gone down. Only a handful heard directly that they should leave. "There definitely were firefighters that we were picking up on the way down that had no knowledge," said Lt. Warren Smith of Ladder 9. "They were, like, they didn't believe us."

"Definitely, the sense of urgency was a huge factor in your ability to get out of there," Lieutenant Smith said. "I don't know what you could attest that to. Experience? Knowledge of the fact that the other building went down; did you have that knowledge? I don't think a lot of guys did."

On the 35th floor, Lt. Gregg Hansson of Engine 24 had just spoken with Battalion Chief Richard Picciotto, when a cry of "Mayday! Evacuate the building" came over the chief's radio. "I get about halfway down the hall and the building starts shaking," Lieutenant Hansson said in an interview.

Chief Picciotto hollered "Mayday!" to the four other fire companies on the 35th floor. Lieutenant Hansson and his men went to Staircase A. In the stairwell, they saw Lt. John Fischer of Ladder 20, who noticed that two of his men had continued up. "He couldn't get them on the radio, so he went to walk up and go get them," Lieutenant Hansson said. "I said, 'All right, well I'm going down, I'm taking my men down.' And that's the last time I saw him."

Somewhere around the 28th or 30th floor, Firefighter Campagna, who had kept climbing after the first tower fell, ran into a crowd of resting firefighters. "A chief came down from a floor above with another company and said, 'Everybody evacuate, everybody out now,'" he recalled. Firefighter Campagna and his company, Engine 28, turned around, and all survived.

Lieutenant Hansson stopped at the 27th floor to pick up a firefighter who had stayed with a man in a wheelchair and his friend. Then Capt. William Burke Jr. of Engine 21 arrived. "Somehow, it was decided that Captain Burke was going to take them down," the lieutenant said. The captain and the two men were killed.

As the court officers made their way down, they were hearing urgent evacuation messages through police officers' radios, Sergeant Wender said. On the 19th floor, they came upon a sight they recall vividly. "The hallway was filled with firemen," Sergeant Wender said. "Some of them were lying down. Ax against the wall. Legs extended. Arm resting against their oxygen tank. Completely exhausted. It led me to believe they were not hearing what we were hearing."

Chief Baccellieri recalled seeing "at least 100 of them." When he shouted that rescuers were evacuating, no one moved. "They said, 'We'll come down in a few minutes,'" Chief Baccellieri said. "These firemen had no idea that the south tower collapsed."

Sergeant Moscola also said they did not move quickly when urged to go. "They said, 'Yeah, all right, we'll be right there.'"

Fire Lieutenant Hansson stopped on this floor, but recalled seeing about 25 people, most of them firefighters. "An unknown firefighter pops out of the hallway, and says, 'I need some help. We've got a lot of people on the other part of the floor who aren't leaving.'" One firefighter pointed to the devastation out the window. "I don't think we can get out," Lieutenant Hansson said the firefighter told him.

Lieutenant Hansson said he urged them to leave, and thought some listened. "In my mind, people weren't moving quick enough for what I thought was necessary," he said. "I had the benefit of knowing that there was an evacuation, that there was a Mayday. Other people didn't hear that."

As Firefighter Campagna passed through the lobby, he saw more firefighters. "Everyone is standing there, waiting to hear what's going to happen next, what's going on," he said. As the court officers passed through the lobby, they saw about 10 firefighters. "We made it by seconds," said Sergeant Moscola.

Near the lobby, Lieutenant Hansson and his men helped remove a heavy man with some Port Authority police officers. They tied the man to a chair with a belt. They barely made it through the door when the tower began collapsing.

Among those who escaped with little time to spare was Susan Frederick. After descending from the 80th floor to about the third, she found the stairway blocked. Behind her, some three dozen people stretched up the stairs.

Minutes later, word spread, person to person, up the line, Ms. Frederick said: "We found a way out." A firefighter had broken through an office wall with an ax.

Daylight filtered faintly through the hole, pointing to the mezzanine and the street.

"Come this way—move quickly!" the firefighter yelled, Ms. Frederick said. He lighted the path with his flashlight. As she made it onto the street, she glanced at her watch, she recalled. It was 10:24 a.m., four minutes before the north tower collapsed. The firefighter did not exit with them.

"He stayed there because there were more people behind us," she said.

22

Report on 9/11 Finds
Flaws in Response
of Police Dept.

William K. Rashbaum

The New York Police Department's response to the Sept. 11 attack was
effective in many areas but suffered from lapses in leadership and coordination and a lack of proper planning and training, according to a draft
report by an independent consultant for the department.

The frank assessment by the consultant, McKinsey & Company, said that
many officers did not know who was in charge or whom they should report
to after the attack. It also said that some officers in the field acted without
direction from field commanders.

The report also found that before Sept. 11, the department's disaster plans
in large measure failed to take into account a possible terrorist attack, that the
police performed few large-scale drills and simulations, and that senior leaders
received little disaster-response training.

The report, however, is measured in its findings, noting that no one could
have anticipated Sept. 11 and that the department performed many tasks ad-
mirably. While leadership lapses, ineffective planning and a lack of coordination at the scene were among the most serious flaws, they did not affect what
many considered to be the department's primary goal that day: the effective
evacuation of the World Trade Center, saving thousands of lives.

Still, the draft is unblinking in its assessment of the lapses that day. While
providing few details or examples, it concluded that the response suffered from

The New York Times, July 27, 2002, "Report on 9/11 Finds Flaws in Response of Police
Dept. (New York Police Department)" by William K. Rashbaum. © 2002 The New
York Times Company. Reprinted with permission.

a "perceived lack of a single strong operational leader" and "unclear roles and responsibilities among some senior leadership."

Those conclusions were based in part on interviews with more than 100 department commanders and officers, a survey of 700 more officers of varying ranks and a review of documents, including internal reports and radio transmissions. In its survey, the consultants found, for example, that 38 percent of officers who went to Lower Manhattan said that they were unsure to whom they should report.

But the 88-page draft, a copy of which was obtained by The New York Times, does not single out any individual police official for praise or criticism. It was based on four months of research by the consulting firm, which traditionally reviews management practices. The company is performing a similar review for the Fire Department.

Even as it addressed flaws—what it called shortfalls—the report noted the heroic performance of so many officers and the department's own sacrifices. "Twenty-three members of the N.Y.P.D. gave their own lives on that day," the report said. "Nothing in this report is intended to detract from the courageous actions."

Deputy Commissioner Michael P. O'Looney, the department's chief spokesman, refused to discuss the report, which is expected to be released next week by Mayor Michael R. Bloomberg and Police Commissioner Raymond W. Kelly. Top department officials and key mayoral aides have already been briefed on the report's conclusions.

"The mayor is traveling, and we don't have a comment," said William Cunningham, Mr. Bloomberg's director of communications.

A spokeswoman for former Mayor Rudolph W. Giuliani, Sunny Mindel, also declined comment on his behalf. "We can't respond to a report that we have not seen that was leaked to The New York Times," she said.

Last night, Bernard B. Kerik, who was police commissioner at the time of the attack and served until the end of Mr. Giuliani's term on Dec. 31, could not be reached for comment. But one senior police official who was involved in the response played down the criticism in the report. "Every day police officers are faced with unimaginable situations, and every day they adapt and survive and do their jobs," he said. Noting that 25 percent of the officers queried in the report were unsatisfied with their supervision that day, the official said that on most days, more than half of the department's officers would say the same thing.

Billed as a forward-looking report, the document is filled with recommendations on how the department could improve its response to a future event of this scope. Officers should be directed to staging areas instead of flooding the scene itself, the report said. More expansive and frequent emergency drills should be undertaken to prepare for the next major catastrophe and better analysis should be performed afterward.

Reserve officers should be held in check in case of a secondary attack, and the department needs to have greater coordination with other agencies like the Fire Department and federal and state authorities, the report said.

Analysts have noted that fire and police commanders barely spoke that day to share information or coordinate strategy. Many of the firefighters who died in the collapse of the second tower were unaware that the first tower had fallen, according to interviews.

"Solving all internal improvement opportunities will not, by itself, be enough," the report said.

Despite what it called the perceived lack of a strong commander and confusion among some top officials, the report found overall that the department acted effectively in 10 of what it described as the 16 critical tasks, including the rescue of civilians, the evacuation of Lower Manhattan, traffic management, and the protection of sensitive locations around the city.

It also said the police radio system performed well, although some officials relied too heavily on cellphones, which the attack knocked out.

At the same time it found what it termed shortfalls in the search for and rescue of survivors after the collapse, assessing the potential risks of hazardous materials at the trade center site and possible secondary attacks, policing the disaster scene, and, perhaps most significantly, assessing and preventing further terrorist threats to the city.

The report also found that field commanders underused the department's command center at 1 Police Plaza and could not sufficiently deploy officers.

While the report said the department performed the pre-collapse rescue and evacuation effectively, it said the post-collapse search for survivors "proved extremely risky given the lack of equipment, training and supervision" among the responders. It also found that intelligence efforts were not well coordinated. There was "no central point for collation and systemic analysis of information regarding the incident, with leaders acting largely on personal observations."

The second half of the report chronicles the perceptions of the officers interviewed or surveyed about how the department responded or should improve. Nearly half, for example, said they would like better rescue and evacuation training. Only 20 percent said they felt confident that the department had developed adequate plans to respond to emergencies. The rest of those polled said they either lacked such confidence or did not have an opinion.

23

Expanding Federal Power: The Real Lessons of Hurricane Katrina

New Government Programs Mean Expanded Federal Powers and Increased Dependence on Government

Steven Yates

Hurricane Katrina was in many ways a disaster of nearly unprecedented proportions for the United States. To be sure, we have suffered disasters before. San Francisco was heavily damaged by an earthquake and a fire in 1906. Chicago succumbed to a raging fire set off, according to urban legend of the time, by the unfortunate Mrs. O'Leary's cow. Galveston was destroyed by a hurricane in 1900. In terms of death toll, however, Katrina remains the worst natural disaster in American history.

Katrina, though, was special, if that word may be used to describe the horrendous damage wrought by the storm. It destroyed not only life and limb, but also damaged and shuttered much of the nation's critical energy infrastructure, caused the submergence and unprecedented abandonment of one of the world's truly great cities (itself a strategically important port city), and obliterated, literally, communities throughout the region. The damage was so great, so terrible, that many questioned the very idea of rebuilding.

The tragedy of the 2005 hurricane season, though, is not confined to its immediate effects on lives and property. The unprecedented scale of disaster has created a similarly unprecedented opportunity for those who would seek to expand the power and reach of the federal government. The Bush

From *The New American*, Vol. 21, Issue 23 (November 14, 2005). Reprinted with permission from The New American.

administration, in fact, is now doing its best to emulate the left-wing socialism of a previous Texan administration, that of Lyndon Johnson. As Bush told the nation on September 15, his administration is planning not only to subsidize the physical rebuilding of affected areas, but also the social reconstruction of the region.

"When communities are rebuilt, they must be even better and stronger than before the storm," Bush said. (Emphasis added.) "Within the Gulf region are some of the most beautiful and historical places in America. As all of us saw on television, there's also some deep, persistent poverty in this region as well. That poverty has roots in a history of racial discrimination, which cut off generations from the opportunity of America. We have a duty to confront this poverty with bold action."

Before confronting any such problem, it is necessary to make a clear-eyed evaluation of the situation. This, of course, is not being done by the Bush administration in its overbearing eagerness to recreate the Johnson administration's "Great Society." Nevertheless, the situation must be evaluated, if not by the Bush administration, then by citizens who will be affected by the government's actions.

There are, in fact, lessons to be learned from the hurricane and its aftermath. First, the ongoing federal war on poverty destroys initiative and creates a dangerous dependence on the federal government that can lead to both paralysis and anarchy during times of crisis. Moreover, the ongoing federal social-welfare programs, instead of eliminating poverty, actually tend to create more poverty, for the simple reason that whatever you subsidize increases in quantity. Second, government is most responsive when its various functions are handled at the lowest level, as close to the people as possible, the appropriate level depending on the specifics of what needs to be done. This must be determined by those present at the problem; it can't be decided within a distant bureaucracy a thousand miles away.

THE ADMINISTRATION'S PLAN

For those who have paid any attention whatsoever to the Bush administration since it first took office, there has never been any doubt about its true nature. Republicans and movement conservatives have been eager to depict Bush as a solidly conservative leader. This has never been true, of course. Since taking office, Bush has done nearly everything he can to expand the powers of government. From the No Child Left Behind Act, which put the Fed in the schools to an unprecedented degree (recall that even Reagan once gave lip service to the idea of abolishing the Federal Department of Education), to new initiatives to put men on the Moon and on Mars, to the diabolically open-ended and misused "War on Terrorism," Bush has sought to expand government at every turn. Katrina has provided Bush another opportunity for federal expansion.

President Bush has called for bold federal action to rebuild New Orleans and surrounding communities on the Gulf Coast in the wake of the devastation wrought by Hurricanes Katrina and Rita. In his September 15 speech, the president urged the creation of three new federal programs. He first proposed a "Gulf Opportunity Zone." According to the president, "Within this zone, we should provide immediate incentives for job-creating investment, tax relief for small businesses, incentives to companies that create jobs, and loans and loan guarantees for small businesses, including minority-owned enterprises, to get them up and running again."

Bush next suggested creating Worker Recovery Accounts for evacuees. Under these, "the federal government would provide accounts of up to $5,000 which these evacuees could draw upon for job training and education to help them get a good job, and for child care expenses during their job search." Finally, he recommended that Congress pass an Urban Homesteading Act under which "we will identify property in the region owned by the federal government, and provide building sites to low-income citizens free of charge through a lottery. In return, they would pledge to build on the lot, with either a mortgage or help from a charitable organization like Habitat for Humanity."

Of course, to accomplish all this and to ensure that no disaster cripples part of the nation ever again, the federal government needs more power to respond to emergencies. Explained Mr. Bush: "Our cities must have clear and up-to-date plans for responding to natural disasters, and disease outbreaks, or a terrorist attack, for evacuating large numbers of people in an emergency, and for providing the food and water and security they would need. In a time of terror threats and weapons of mass destruction, the danger to our citizens reaches much wider than a fault line or a flood plain. I consider detailed emergency planning to be a national security priority, and therefore, I've ordered the Department of Homeland Security to undertake an immediate review, in cooperation with local counterparts, of emergency plans in every major city in America." Naturally, Bush made no mention of which section of the Constitution authorizes the federal government to either manage local disasters or conduct reviews of municipalities' disaster policies and procedures.

As radical as this vision is, Bush still wasn't through. In his post-Katrina America, U.S. armed forces could conceivably turn the nation into a garrison state—for our own protection, of course. After noting the lack of coordination in the response to Katrina by the Federal Emergency Management Agency (FEMA), Bush issued his most controversial call: "It is now clear that a challenge on this scale requires greater federal authority and a broader role for the armed forces—the institution of our government most capable of massive logistical operations on a moment's notice." To that end, Bush ordered his cabinet secretaries to review the federal response to the disaster. "This government will learn the lessons of Hurricane Katrina," Bush promised (or warned, depending on your perspective). "We're going to review every action and make necessary changes, so that we are better prepared for any challenge of nature, or act of evil men, that could threaten our people."

How much is all this going to cost? The cost to liberty will be incalculable. In dollars, Congress immediately appropriated $61.8 billion in emergency relief. But this is only the start. One Congressional Budget Office estimate places the total cost of rebuilding the region as high as $200 billion. FEMA will get $60 billion, portions of which are already contracted to corporations such as the Shaw Group ($100 million) and Bechtel ($100 million), among others, for reconstruction work. Another $400 million will go to the Army Corps of Engineers. Another $1.9 billion will go to the Department of Defense for repairs on damaged bases. Since Bush refuses to raise taxes, all the money will be borrowed mostly from foreign central banks, which means that the national debt will go up even higher (it has reached $8 trillion as of this writing). Bush, however, pledged, "We will do what it takes" to rebuild the area—the hundreds of buildings, roads, bridges, and businesses that dot the area.

THE NEWLY VISIBLE UNDERCLASS

Just prior to Katrina, the U.S. Census Bureau released figures indicating that since the turn of the millennium, poverty in America has been increasing. According to these figures, as of 2004 some 37 million Americans lived in poverty—over a million more than in 2003.

This poverty had a role to play in the Katrina disaster. At first, it was mystifying that so many people did not flee New Orleans, knowing that the storm was coming. Katrina hit, and the next day, the levees built to withstand only a Category Three storm broke. This flooded the city and stranded thousands of people without food, electricity, or clean water. Why were these people still in New Orleans? Because nearly 30 percent of those living in the city were beneath the poverty line. They had no way out. Their number included the sick, the elderly, and the disabled as well as many of what quickly became a newly visible underclass. They didn't own cars or have familial or social networks enabling them to escape. The social safety net failed. While reports of atrocities by roving gangs (rapes, for example) appear to have been gross exaggerations, New Orleans and the surrounding area suddenly took on the appearance of something out of a third-world nation.

How could this have happened after decades of federal efforts aimed, supposedly, at the eradication of poverty? Such a question can't be answered without revisiting the hoary debate over the causes of poverty, about which liberals and conservatives have traditionally lined up on opposite sides of a now very rusty fence. How much poverty is due to poverty-inducing behaviors, and how much is due to circumstances beyond the person's control? And do top-down government actions tend to reduce or actually encourage poverty by rewarding poverty-inducing behaviors?

Most human social reality has more than one cause, and poverty is no exception. People can end up poor through no fault of their own. A

manufacturing plant that provided jobs to thousands but then closes and relo-
cates overseas in order to take advantage of cheap labor leaves poverty behind
in the region it once called home. Standards of living immediately drop when
new jobs pay just a fraction of the old or come without health benefits. The
"working poor" usually cannot afford private health insurance. An unanticipated illness causing a long period with no income can precipitate financial
disaster for an individual or a family.

Why are there so many "working poor" in this tragic situation? The main
reason is the absence of jobs that pay wages sufficient to lift them above the
poverty line. A specific factor we can look at here is the so-called North American Free Trade Agreement (NAFTA). According to the Economic Policy
Institute, some one million U.S. jobs have been displaced since NAFTA went
into effect on January 1, 1994. Two-thirds of these jobs were in manufacturing
industries, although every major occupation was affected in every state in the
union. NAFTA's defenders contend that it created jobs, but the "service sector"
jobs (customer service representatives, telemarketers, waiters and waitresses,
and the notorious burger flippers) paid far less than what was displaced.

In concert with the NAFTA-induced exodus of jobs has been a corre-
sponding influx of illegal aliens competing with American workers for scarce
jobs. Our current immigration crisis can be traced to the Immigration Act of
1965, which made it easier for non-Europeans to cross our borders legally.
There is nothing fundamentally wrong with immigration so long as immigrants respect the rule of law and are willing to assimilate, learn English, and
adapt to American culture. In recent decades, however, the trickle of illegal
immigrants became a flood that has increased to the point where thousands
are crossing our border from Mexico every day. They are working in jobs that
would otherwise be held by Americans. Because of their illegal status, they are
willing also to work for low pay and no benefits, thus driving down wages for
Americans. But they are here because of the absence of jobs in Mexico.
NAFTA is part of this story, too. An anonymous illegal alien from Mexico
once commented in an interview, "If NAFTA had worked, we wouldn't
be here."

Many of the welfare programs introduced during the "war on poverty" of
the 1960s had the predictable result of making poverty intractable. In launch-
ing what was then called an "unconditional war on poverty in America," the
Johnson administration expanded Medicare and created Aid to Families with
Dependent Children, Head Start, the Job Corps, and Medicaid. The Nixon
administration continued or expanded these programs. The welfare state bur-
geoned. Instead of ending poverty, however, these programs institutionalized
it by creating dependency. Charles Murray, author of such well-known books
as *Losing Ground,* wrote that "the expansions in public welfare... led to disin-
centives to work, a corruption of values and thus welfare resulted in more
welfare."

Murray understood that if you believe the federal government is going to
take care of you, you'll behave accordingly. And since the 1960s, millions of

people have come to expect government to take care of them through welfare programs like Aid to Families with Dependent Children. People dependent on government largesse for their welfare become unable to care for themselves. In the South as Katrina approached, this created a dangerous and deadly situation. In the end, thousands of people were unable to do anything to help themselves when disaster struck on August 29. Instead, they waited for the federal government to come to the rescue! Yet, as Bush conceded, the federal response was inept and inadequate, as—befitting a lethargic, distant bureaucracy—it was bound to be.

Of course, the tragedy was not alone to be found in the poor who were left defenseless in the wake of nature's wrath. The tragedy too was that government intervention, when it came, brought government force. And this is a lesson that needs to be learned.

When the government called in the military, the humanitarian mission in New Orleans became a military operation, and as such, people in the city were treated like subjects of a military occupation rather than as free citizens of a Republic. People were forced against their will to leave their properties. People were forced against their will to remain in dangerously unsanitary holding pens like the Superdome. People were even forced to surrender their firearms. In the face of disaster, the freedoms of the people, the protection of which caused the government to be created in the first place, were squashed by that very government. There is a clear lesson here. When you give the government the power to save, you give the government the power to destroy.

REBUILDING NEW ORLEANS

There is no question that New Orleans must be rebuilt! There must be a port where the great Mississippi flows into the Gulf, and a port cannot exist without a city. New Orleans is a crucial city, historically, culturally, and economically. Because of its importance, abandoning the Big Easy is not an option. Failure to rebuild will leave the nation devoid of one of its most crucial ports, will leave many without the homes and businesses and properties they long to return to, and will leave a nearly irreplaceable void in the nation's cultural life. But who bears responsibility for this rebuilding project? One thing is for sure: it should not be the federal government!

In fact, there is no need for federal involvement, as the response of the private sector to Katrina abundantly illustrates. Arguably, Katrina brought out what has always been best in the American people—their natural empathy and generosity. It is not in the nature of Americans to allow others to suffer without doing something about it. Millions of Americans have donated money, foodstuffs, and clothing to the evacuees who were transported to their cities and towns. Many have donated time and additional effort attempting to see to it that the necessary goods found their way into the hands of those needing them. They have worked through churches, businesses, charitable organizations, and personal networks. Local authorities have seen to it that the evacuees had places to sleep. Schools have opened their doors to their children. What we have seen over the past couple of months is a spontaneous relief effort that emerged from all across the land. It even included large corporations like Wal-Mart.

New Orleans was a sufficiently beloved city that I can visualize many people taking out time and effort to assist in what will doubtless be a colossal rebuilding effort—an effort holding out better hope of building the "better and stronger" New Orleans about which President Bush spoke.

Catholic social thinkers sometimes speak of a principle of subsidiarity—the principle of solving problems at the most local level possible, and only moving to higher levels of governmental authority for problems proving intractable at the local level. Subsidiarity is the principle that should guide us here. Those evacuees who want to return ought to be allowed to direct as much traffic as possible. Those closest to the problems are all too aware of what they lost to the storm and its aftermath, and so are in the best position to know how they want things to look when they are back in place. Subsidiarity also ensures that those at the local level who are engaged in rebuilding their own properties and lives will have the greatest possible degree of control over the decisions they are making. This is the essence of freedom and the beginning of dignity, both of which will be squashed should rebuilding efforts be dictated and controlled by a central authority in Washington.

Nevertheless, many will not accept an approach based on subsidiarity. Of course, those who support welfare-statism will call it heartless, accusing those advocating private solutions of not minding if people flounder helplessly. Nothing could be further from the truth. The evacuees are not on their own? While of course there are countless hours of work still to be done—work that will take months if not years—the work will be done? Federal power, on the other hand, has proven itself to be an extremely blunt instrument.

What could be more heartless than the kinds of stories that emerged from New Orleans during the days when FEMA was in charge? Example: the woman seen sobbing alongside the road when a FEMA official would not allow her to take her dog with her on a bus. Her pet was the one thing she had salvaged from her ruined home, and a government employee with a bureaucratic, follow-the-rules mindset refused to allow her to keep it. Or think of FEMA's notorious refusals to allow shipments of goods from Wal-Mart and the Red Cross to be delivered. Or FEMA's blocking off all exits from the ruined city. Speaking more generally, wouldn't it be more heartless for the federal government to keep in place all the programs that brought about the cycles of poverty whose effects were evident in the wrecked New Orleans?

The idea of allowing the American people to act spontaneously to rebuild New Orleans and the other ruined communities on the Gulf Coast will not sit well with the bureaucratic mind. It would mean taking control away from those who ardently desire to exercise control over the lives of others. It will seem simplistic and messy to them: simplistic because it trusts the essential goodness of the American people and their capacity to respond to the suffering of others, messy because it won't assume the kind of centralization that has been falling into place over the past several decades. But people will have the dignity that comes with the freedom to make their own choices. And their choices will be better absent the graft and waste always associated with government projects; they will achieve far more for less money; and absent federally subsidized flood insurance, they will be less likely to build in high-risk areas—and thereby avoid the horrific devastation that always occurs in those areas whenever the next hurricane rolls through.

THE DANGER AHEAD

Hurricane Katrina revealed poverty and desperation—but also the natural generosity and kindness of Americans who have never been willing to let others suffer needlessly. It also revealed the inherent weakness of centralization and, alarmingly, it revealed also an administration eager to justify the assumption of new, and potentially abusive, powers. The real lessons of Katrina are that acts of power, exercised in top-down fashion by the federal government, are not the way to go.

In the wake of the storm, Bush promised "one of the largest reconstruction efforts the world has ever seen." The federal response to Katrina can be seen as an instance of this administration's overriding tendency to respond to each new crisis with a call for more power. The 9/11 attacks saw the creation of the Orwellian Homeland Security Agency and the draconian USA Patriot Act. Both have since been expanded by new legislation from a Congress willing to go right along with the president. Earlier this year we saw the passage of the Real ID Act, which arguably gives every U.S. citizen a national ID in 2008. If you go back and read the president's September 15 speech closely, you will notice that it isn't just about this emergency. He is looking for expanded powers to deal with any and all emergencies, real or imagined. He has since called for the potential use of the military to quarantine entire cities, should there be outbreaks here of the much-talked-about bird flu. This would set a precedent for nothing less than martial law in America—and on the basis of a state of affairs that may never come to pass!

Warnings that the current administration is seeking dangerously expanded federal powers are often met with "so what" shrugs from "conservatives" who are quick to say that this president will not abuse such powers. It should be remembered, though, that powers granted during one administration may wind up abused by another. Indeed, it is not any particular administration that one must fear. What is to be feared is the accumulation of power.

Our Founding Fathers created constitutional government limiting federal power to a few, carefully specified functions for a specific reason: they believed concentrations of power were dangerous. They knew that unless they were kept on a short leash, governments tended to accumulate power. Some of them warned how fragile liberty really is. "The natural progress of things," wrote Thomas Jefferson, "is for liberty to yield and government to gain ground." They wanted to avoid the very thing that had compelled them to fight for independence against the British Empire. It did not occur to the Founding Fathers that government should institute large programs designed to provide the poor with safety nets, or involve itself in education, or in medicine, or in any of the other endeavors it has involved itself with during the intervening 200-plus years. Federal disaster relief, federal authority to quarantine cities, federal authority to grant a national ID: none of these things were contemplated by the Founding Fathers as legitimate aspects of federal authority, and nowhere in the Constitution can one find any legal authorization for Washington to involve itself in these matters.

The passage of time, though, can make men forgetful. As a nation, we have forgotten the wisdom of the Founding Fathers and rushed headlong to create a welfare state. That welfare state is part of the reason, a big part, why Hurricane Katrina caused so many people so much trouble. Now our present state of affairs is such that when a hurricane strikes a major city the result is infrastructural collapse. We are arguably worse off today than we were half a century ago despite all the advances in technology. Now, the Bush administration wants to use Katrina to justify further dangerous expansions of federal power and of the welfare state. For the good of the nation, for the good of generations to come, Congress must be convinced not to go along with this scheme.

Steven Yates, Ph.D., teaches philosophy at the University of South Carolina Upstate (located in Spartanburg, S.C.) and Greenville Technical College (located in Greenville, S.C.).

24

Improving Emergency Responsiveness with Management Science

Linda V. Green and Peter J. Kolesar

W hile the goal of OR/MS is to aid decision makers, implementation of published models occurs less frequently than one might hope. However, one area that has been significantly impacted by management science is emergency response systems. Dozens of papers on emergency service management appeared in the OR/MS literature in the 1970s alone, many of which were published in *Management Science*. Three of these papers won major prizes. More importantly, many of these papers led to the implementation of substantially new policies and practices, particularly in policing and firefighting. Much of this work originated in New York City, though many other cities subsequently adopted the resulting models and strategies. In this paper, we look at the context, content, and nature of the research and the factors that led to these early implementation successes. We then track the extent to which these original models are still affecting decision making in emergency response systems. We also examine the pace of development of new OR/MS models and applications in the area. Finally, we look at issues in emergency responsiveness that have emerged recently as a result of the national focus on terrorism and discuss the potential for future OR/MS modeling and application.

Management Science, August 2004 v50 i8 p1001(14) "Improving Emergency Responsiveness with Management Science" by Linda V. Green and Peter J. Kolesar. © 2004 Institute for Operations Research and the Management Sciences.

INTRODUCTION

In his editorial mission statement for this journal, Wally Hopp stated that "Management Science needs to play a leadership role in applying our legacy of powerful analytic tools to high-level, long-term planning issues faced by managers" (Hopp 2003, p. v). One area that has enjoyed considerable success in this regard is emergency response systems. Beginning in the late 1960s, papers on the allocation and deployment of police, fire, and ambulance resources that provided important insights, policies, and procedures for managers began to appear in this journal with regularity. This activity continued through the 1970s and into the 1980s. A large fraction of the models in these papers were actually implemented, particularly in New York City, which sponsored much of the basic research; and, many of the models and resulting policies were subsequently used in other cities and had lasting impact on practice.

As the public sector applications department of *Management Science* is the only department of the journal that contains the word "applications" in its title, we thought it fitting that this paper, written for the journal's 50th anniversary, focus on this era of application success, examine the factors that led to it, and trace the legacy of these publications and models on practice as well as on research. Our intention is not to provide a comprehensive literature survey (see Kolesar and Swersey 1986, Swersey 1994) but rather to give a more personal overview of the developments and impact of this body of work, taking advantage of our own involvement in its history. We also highlight the role of *Management Science* itself in publishing much of the best of these analyses. In doing so, we hope to provide some insight on the elements of successful model development, implementation, and dissemination in the public sector. And, we feel that it is equally important to examine how and why some of these once-successful models have faded from use while others continue to be implemented, although sometimes in limited ways. Finally, we observe the relative scarcity of papers on emergency services in recent years and ask whether the new attention on homeland security and emergency preparedness may presage renewed interest and activity in model development and application in this area.

HISTORY

The late 1960s was a time of unrest in the United States. National crime statistics were rising steadily and Barry Goldwater, the Republican presidential candidate in the 1964 presidential election, made "crime in the streets" a major campaign issue. The assassination of Martin Luther King in 1968 and the civil unrest that followed, the takeovers of a number of universities, including notably our own home institution, Columbia, and the sometimes violent and always turbulent protests over the war in Vietnam, impressively exemplified in the massive protests at the Democratic Party's national convention in Chicago 1968, were all features of the times.

Simultaneously, in some circles, there was optimism about the potential of computer models and mathematical analysis for solving public policy issues. The Apollo space missions were underway, culminating in the first manned lunar landing, in 1969. Many commentators asked in full earnestness, "If we can land a man on the moon, why can't we . . . ?" The implication was that similar analytical thinking and technology should be used to attack fundamental social problems. The field of OR/MS was still young and many of its practitioners and leaders had either participated in the original World War II military work that the field was rooted in, or had been trained by those pioneers. They shared the heady feeling that mathematical modeling could be applied to many of the nation's problems.

In the domain of public safety and emergency services, two political initiatives were particularly influential and productive. The first we mention only briefly. In response to Candidate Goldwater's charges about crime in America, President Lyndon Johnson in 1965 established The President's Commission on Law Enforcement and the Administration of Justice. The Commission's Science and Technology Task Force was chaired by Alfred Blumstein, then of the Institute for Defense Analyses and an influential figure in the OR/MS community, having served as president of ORSA, TIMS, and INFORMS. The Science and Technology Task Force was charged with exploring how computer modeling and technology could be utilized in attacking crime. Only a small part of its work was related to operational policing issues, but that little amount was noteworthy in that it jumpstarted the career of Richard Larson, then a graduate student at MIT, whose work with the commission contributed to his Lanchester Prize-winning book *Urban Police Patrol Analysis* (Larson 1972). (Larson has also served as president of ORSA and INFORMS.) Overviews of the work of the Technology Task Force on the modeling of criminal careers, the impact of incarceration, etc. may be found in the papers of Blumstein (2002), Larson (2002), and Maltz (1994).

The second political initiative, The New York City-RAND Institute (NYCRI), had a more profound impact on the development of emergency service deployment modeling. The institute was a unique partnership between the City of New York and the RAND Corporation of Santa Monica, California. RAND was the original and prototypical military think tank; a direct outgrowth of the first operations research work done for the U.S. Air Force during World War II. (1) By the late 1960s, RAND had started to broaden its portfolio of work into domestic policy research in areas such as telecommunications, education and human resources, and energy.

Here is a thumbnail sketch of how and why the NYCRI came about. (2) John V. Lindsay was elected mayor of New York City in 1966 on a platform of governmental reform. To this end, his administration carried out substantial structural city government reforms, including a major reorganization that reduced the number of agencies reporting directly to the mayor from

50 to 12. In what was at that time an original move, Lindsay hired a core of some 50 "analysts/administrators." E. S. (Steve) Savas, originally at IBM and the author of several *Management Science* papers on public sector issues, was one of these analytically trained administrators (Savas 1969, 1973, 1978).

Fredrick O. Hayes, Mayor Lindsay's first budget director and a key figure behind these reforms, was motivated to bring even more analytic competence to bear on city problems with his perception of the "appalling growth rate of virtually all of the problems to which municipal programs and services were directed. Crime, drug use, fire alarms, solid waste . . ." (Hayes 1972, p. 1). This dismal prospect and his faith in analysis led Hayes to request Ford Foundation funding to create a RAND-type institution devoted to the city's problems. When this did not materialize, he went to RAND itself. This chance to diversify out of military work was exactly what RAND was looking for and negotiations led to the formation of the RAND Corporation–New York City partnership in late 1968. While NYCRI would eventually work on diverse problems in many city agencies, the initial research contracts were with the Fire Department, the Housing and Development Administration (largely public housing and administration of the city's rent control laws) the Police Department, and Health Services (primarily the administration of the municipal hospital system).

While the institute's formal status with the city was that of a contractor, from the outset both the city and RAND saw this as more than the usual consultancy. The relationship with RAND was to be long term and comprehensive, focusing on immediate problems as well as on those that would require sustained study, experimentation, change and reevaluation. Mayor Lindsay spoke of the " . . . willingness on the part of RAND to leave model building long enough to assist in the application of their new systems in a real agency in a real city" (Dickson 1971, p. 249). On the other hand, NYCRI's first president wrote that the researchers should be "insulated enough from city hall's daily operational concerns to work persistently on underlying problems" (Szanton 1972, p. 20).

However, the political landscape of New York was not simple, and having the mayor and his budget director as enthusiastic clients did not itself make the going easy. By hiring RAND without their prior consultation, the mayor had in effect imposed RAND on the city agencies. Some in the agencies saw the RAND researchers as spies for City Hall. One of RAND's political scientists and the second leader of the RAND Fire Project observed, "Since the consultant must have information . . . and often only the bureaucracy has that information, by selectively cooperating with the consultant, the bureaucracy can effectively scuttle the desired change" (Archibald and Hoffman 1969, p. 10). The city's chief financial officer, Comptroller Abraham Beame, had been the mayoral candidate whom Lindsay had defeated. Beame's opposition to the institute was not concealed. He was a supporter of the political status quo and his view, shared by many, was that anything RAND was doing, if it were indeed worth doing, could be done more cheaply by professors at the

City University of New York. The City Council, the legislative branch of city government, had to approve the RAND contracts and soon demanded a voice in shaping the research agenda. The city's powerful municipal worker labor unions quickly accused the institute of being little more than stop-watch carrying, antiworker efficiency experts. Before long, left-leaning commentators portrayed the RAND researchers as a collection of cold-blooded Dr. Strangeloves who would have the city burn down at the altar of cost-effectiveness modeling (Hoos 1972, Wallace and Wallace 1999). Indeed, some of this criticism made its way to the pages of this very journal (Wallace and Wallace 1980, Chaiken et al. 1980).

To a considerable extent the RAND strategy was to stay out of the limelight and try to make other people look good. But this could backfire too. After several years of generally successful work, the institute recognized that it had no constituency outside of the mayor's office. Moreover, a credit/blame game developed in which even the successful Fire Project researchers felt that the New York Fire Department (FDNY) chose to take credit for itself, or let RAND take blame according to its own convenience. In this environment, it is remarkable that anything positive was achieved by "systems analysis and management science."

THE RAND FIRE PROJECT

One of the initial NYCRI contracts with the city was with the FDNY, a project that began at the very start of the RAND–New York City relationship in January 1968 and lasted until the institute's doors closed in September 1975. The Fire Project was, by many accounts, the most successful of the NYCRI ventures. The FDNY's problems were very painful. In the five years from 1963 to 1968, fire alarms in New York City increased 96% from 116,000 to 227,000, while firefighting resources stayed almost constant. FDNY operating expenses were increasing at over 20% per year, largely as a consequence of wage increases for its 14,000 uniformed firefighters. Workloads on individual firemen were excessive, with some fire companies responding to alarms more than 8,000 times a year, or nearly once an hour, 24 hours a day, 365 days a year. During peak times, some fire companies ran from one incident to another all night long. Dennis Smith's best-selling book, *Report from Engine Company 82*, gives a compelling picture of the stress and danger the firefighters faced at this time (Smith 1969).

The fire communications system, still the same telegraphic-driven bell system that had been designed when fire engines were horse-drawn, was becoming severely congested. Everyone's "pet solution" was to bring technology to the rescue: "Let's get a new high-tech communications system for FDNY." This was to be RAND's first mission. But before too long, the researchers found that communications problems, while real, were not quite what they were originally thought to be, nor would an efficient solution be automatically achieved by "a big computer in the sky" (Greenberger et al. 1976, Chapters 7 and 8). While important queuing analyses were being done on immediate communications bottlenecks by project member Arthur Swersey, the RAND team got FDNY support for its view that resource deployment and fire incidence forecasting were fundamental issues that needed intensive study. The Fire Project was initially staffed primarily by RAND military systems analysts from Santa Monica. When it was realized that OR/MS work would be at the core of the project, RAND began to recruit additional management scientists locally. First Ed Ignall and Art Swersey, and then Peter Kolesar and Kenneth Rider, all of Columbia University, joined the project team. The project staff also included Warren Walker, Jan Chaiken, and Edward Blum, RAND-based researchers who were hired directly into the New York City office. Most of the academics would at some point take extended leaves of absence from their home institutions to work on the Fire Project full time.

The nature of the fire problems, the state of the art of OR/MS research on emergency services, and the proclivities of the researchers led to a particular style of working. First, there was essentially no existing OR/MS literature, so the researchers had to start afresh. (Exceptions, like the papers of Valinsky 1955 and Hogg 1968, were of limited use.) The team, which had a pragmatic orientation, went to fires with the firefighters, slept over in firehouses, sat at the shoulders of the dispatchers in the communications center, poured over fatal fire reports in the archives, and, most importantly, cleaned up the fire data tapes. Although the FDNY had created computerized records of all fire alarms for the five years prior to the start of the project, the data had never been analyzed; the piles of punch cards were in terrible shape and it took months of work to get these records cleaned up and into a format in which they could be used for analysis.

The first major piece of management science work done by the RAND team was the creation of a simulation model of firefighting operations (Carter and Ignall 1970; Walker et al. 1979, Chapter 13). Development of this model received highest priority as real-life experimentation with the fire system, such as changes in dispatch strategies, the communication system, or the number of fire companies on duty, would be too expensive or dangerous. Technical aspects of the design of the fire simulation model were innovative and influential (Carter and Ignall 1975), and it proved to be the foundation on which both specific new deployment tactics (Kolesar and Walker 1974, Ignall et al. 1982) and general new theories (Kolesar and Blum 1973) were validated.

Although the research team eschewed theoretical formulations for their own sake, much of the early work on these issues had a distinctly theoretical OR/MS flavor: queueing models of fire company availability (Chaiken and Ignall 1972, Carter et al. 1972); an empirical Bayes' approach to alarm forecasting (Carter and Rolph 1973, 1974); a stochastically based integer linear programming formulation of fire company relocations (Kolesar and Walker 1974); and Markovian decision models of initial dispatch to a new alarm (Swersey 1982, Ignall et al. 1982). While each piece of work contributed to the researchers' understanding of fire deployment, the sophisticated models were generally not the most important contributions to actual operations. There were two dominant reasons for this. First, many of the problems that intrigued the researchers from an analytical perspective were tactical and had limited impact. One such example was identification of the fire companies that would constitute an optimal initial dispatch to a new alarm of unknown severity. The elegant stochastic formulation that was developed for this rather micro problem only made sense in the most stressed neighborhoods of New York City, as it focused on the phenomenon of random fire company unavailability that was at the heart of the dispatch dilemma in these neighborhoods. Second, the insights obtained from the more sophisticated models could often be translated into simple heuristics or rules. For example, ideas emanating from the research on initial dispatching were implemented as simple ranked lists of high-priority alarm boxes in the most stressed neighborhoods (Ignall et al. 1975).

Such tactical issues were not as vital to senior FDNY management as the broader questions of how many fire companies were really needed in New York City, and where should they be located to provide fair and adequate protection to neighborhoods as diverse as the Wall Street financial district, the Upper East Side, Harlem, and the suburbs of eastern Queens. These macro issues involving millions of dollars eventually succumbed to much simpler, often deterministic, models. A prime example is the "firehouse-siting model," which was the simplest of all the models developed, but also the most influential and enduring. It took the RAND team a while to understand that simple models would work, though. One could consider the contribution of much of the more elegant work as being partly foundational and partly a side payment to the research team taken in the form of publications in journals such as *Management Science*. It would have been very difficult to keep this talented team together without the prospect of publication in refereed journals as none of the academic members of the team was yet tenured. The research results of the Fire Project were formally reported to the city as a series of RAND Research Reports, or "Rs," many of which are still available in RAND deposit libraries around the world and from RAND's website at http://www.rand.org. (3)

Sometimes theoretical research yielded big payoffs, however. A prime example was the work on fire company travel distances and travel times, which resulted in the square root law (Kolesar and Blum 1973) described in the next section. It was largely motivated by B. O. Koopman's derivation of his logarithmic laws of search effectiveness, which led to a breakthrough in deployment of antisubmarine search forces during World War II. Koopman, a mathematical physicist, had derived his laws of search from physical principles, and they were later confirmed by direct observation (Koopman 1956a, b; 1957). One of the authors, Kolesar, a former student of Koopman's at Columbia, was troubled by the fact that the Fire Project team often resorted to ad hoc detailed calculations of the consequences of alternative polices. After spending countless days in a room at RAND that was wallpapered from floor to ceiling with enormous maps of firehouses and fire locations, he started to wonder: "Why isn't there a simple general law of fire protection that would answer the big questions of where companies should be located and how many there should be?" When Kolesar articulated this musing to Ed Blum, the Fire Project leader, Blum replied at once: "Oh, I know what it is. Response distance goes down with the square root of the number of fire companies." "How do you know that?" Blum responded, "It's simple: Distance is the square root of area." It took months of work to fully develop and test this theory, but in the end it became the cornerstone of many of the most useful analyses done by the team, including its work on the biggest issue of all—determining the number of companies that should be located in each of the FDNY's commands. A move toward analytic simplicity had begun, but was only credible because of the work that had come before, particularly, the development of, and experiments with, the simulation model.

As response time, not response distance, was the key proxy used to evaluate the FDNY's performance, it was important to model fire engine travel velocity. No one inside the FDNY knew how fast engines went and how speed varied by time of day or weather, etc., so the team designed experiments to measure velocities across the city. These were resisted at first by the firefighters' union—some stop watches were thrown against fire house walls or mysteriously dropped off the fire trucks. But, in the end, the data was collected and provided the basis of a nonlinear regression model of fire engine travel time as a function of distance that has since been revalidated in other cities (Kolesar et al. 1975a).

Some of the practical impacts of the Fire Project on New York City are documented in the project's application for the 1974 College on the Practice of Management Science (Edelman) Award, including demonstrated annual savings of $5 million on a base of a $375 million operating budget. The Fire Project was costing the city about $500,000 a year—less than a single fire company. As detailed therein, the team's research played a role in the city's decisions to close six fire companies and permanently relocate seven others, all carried out in 1972 when alarm rates had fallen off a bit and budgetary pressures were increasing. In addition, an "adaptive response" initial dispatch policy had alleviated workload in the high fire-incidence regions of the Bronx and Brooklyn, and the FDNY was planning to implement a dynamic relocation algorithm. Indeed, by 1975, this real-time, integer LP-based relocation algorithm designed by Kolesar and Walker was successfully implemented as part of a new computerized FDNY Management Information and Control System. During the years when New York City's alarm rates were at their peak, the algorithm was used to suggest fire company relocations many times daily.

Over the next several years the pace of work on macro resource-allocation issues quickened as the FDNY was repeatedly called on to contribute cost reductions to the city's efforts to balance its budget. By 1974, the city had entered a severe budget crisis and more fire company closings were explicitly requested by the mayor's office. The RAND models were used to identify those company changes that potentially had the least deleterious impact on fire protection. This happened in several waves and, in total, by 1978 24 fire company locations were closed and 10 of the companies permanently disbanded. These closings were challenged in court by the firefighter's union and the affected neighborhoods. The strong analytic basis underlying the closing decisions was a factor in defeating these lawsuits. At first the analyses were rather ad hoc and employed the square root model to estimate the impact of average response times in the impacted regions. Later, the RAND firehouse-siting model, which was developed in 1975 as the NYCRI was closing, played a central role in the closing decisions (Walker et al. 1979, Chapter 9; Dormont et al. 1975; Walker 1975). Based on a computerized map of all fire alarm boxes and fire company locations in a region, this model computes static response times for each alarm box in that region using historical alarm frequencies and the square root law and travel time models. While many other considerations, some overtly political, came into play, the models were influential. (4) Moreover, to support the continued use of the RAND models and the analysis mission in general, in 1974 the FDNY created a Division of Planning and Operations Research staffed with OR/MS professionals.

There were frustrations as well. For example, the RAND analysts realized early on that there was a gross mismatch between the constant number of fire companies on duty around the clock and the enormous peaking of both false alarms and real fires in the evening hours. A variety of staffing alternatives were devised by the team to improve the hourly match-up between the number of fire companies on duty and the alarm rate, but the strong opposition of the politically powerful firefighters union defeated them all (Ignall et al. 1975, Kolesar and Rider 1981).

On the management science front, the RAND team produced some 15 papers in refereed journals that were directly based on the project's deployment research. Of these, four appeared in *Management Science* while five were published in sister journal *Operations Research*. The work of the team garnered three awards: the 1975 Lanchester Prize of ORSA for the relocation algorithm (Kolesar and Walker 1974); second prize in the 1974 Edelman competition on the practice of management science (Ignall et al. 1975); and the 1976 NATO Systems Science Prize for a collection of 13 technical publications produced by the team between 1970 and 1975. It is noteworthy that, because of their operational and applied nature and the modest number of new theorems they contained, much of this work was difficult to get published in top-tier journals. For example, the Lanchester prize-winning paper on the relocation algorithm was rejected by *Management Science* because, as noted by one referee, "it contains not a single lemma or theorem."

After the initial successes of the Fire Project, the NYCRI was able to obtain modest financial support from the U.S. Department of Housing and Urban Development (HUD) for the dissemination of the institute's research on emergency service deployment to other cities. The methodological legacy

of the project, in addition to the articles scattered through the technical literature, is the book produced by the team members under support from HUD
(Walker et al. 1979). In this book, the authors linked the various stand-alone
journal articles and RAND reports into an organized course on fire deployment analysis. Material was added about the background of fire services,
change management issues, and the like. The level of technical discussion of
the models was targeted to future fire department staff analysts. However,
nothing was oversimplified. It is also noteworthy that the firehouse-siting
model, which would ultimately prove to be so useful in New York City, was
funded by HUD and was initially applied in cities such as Yonkers, New York;
Trenton, New Jersey; Denver, Colorado; and Wilmington, Delaware.

THE POLICE PROJECT

A parallel NYCRI contract was initiated with the New York Police Department (NYPD) when the institute opened in 1968. The Police Project's original scope was not as focused on operational deployment issues as was the work
with the FDNY. Much of the police work in the early years was on "softer"
policy analysis, e.g., minority recruitment, effectiveness of criminal investigations, and police corruption. Alone among the Police Project members,
Richard Larson worked on deployment issues related to the operations of New
York's 911 emergency telephone system dispatching office. His suggestions
were almost immediately implemented (Larson 1972, 2002). Overall, however, there was not the intensive cooperation on deployment that character-
ized RAND's relationship with the FDNY. Personalities and NYPD politics
played a critical role. Whereas the FDNY chief saw the RAND researchers as
allies propelling agendas that were his own, the RAND team was unable to
gain an insider position with the most powerful forces in the NYPD.

During the early NYCRI years, the NYPD was an institution under siege
(Murphy 1977, Daley 1973). There was massive pressure on the department
over the issue of police brutality toward minorities. Then, the devastating police
corruption scandals that surfaced in the Knapp Commission (Knapp 1972)
investigations forced the resignation of Howard Leary, the first police commissioner in office during the Police Project. His replacement was a man who
appeared to think that he personally had all the answers to the department's
problems. The NYPD as a whole was demoralized and defensive. It was not an
environment conducive to research. In addition, it did not help that RAND
was associated with Mayor Lindsay, who had tried to impose an effective civilian review board to oversee citizen complaints of police violence. Under hostile
examination during a city council hearing, the president of the institute testi-
fied that the police commissioner had expected the RAND team to be sea-
soned veterans but complained that key participants were "young MIT
graduates." Further, he stated that, in contrast to what was happening at FDNY,
RAND was telling the police things they did not want to hear (Ranzel 1970).

The so-called "fourth platoon" controversy illustrates how the RAND analysts were stymied in their first year of work with the NYPD. The gross mismatch between how patrol cars were scheduled for duty as compared to the hills and valleys of the daily temporal demand for police services had been noted by the Lindsay administration even before RAND came on the scene. The mayor tried to get the NYPD to implement a corrective "fourth platoon"—an overlay tour on the traditional three "platoons" that worked midnight to 8 a.m., 8 a.m. to 4 p.m., and 4 p.m. to midnight. RAND researchers actually generated one version of a fourth platoon plan, but only the mayor's office was receptive to it.

After the first unsuccessful year, police work at NYCRI went into dormancy with no further NYPD funding, but was modestly sustained by HUD. Then, in 1974, optimistic that the Fire Project team's talents could be equally helpful to the NYPD, RAND reassigned researchers Chaiken, Swersey, Kolesar, and Walker to a renewed Police Project. After new team members rode around in patrol cars, sat in the dispatching center, and scrutinized data from 911 tapes, a detailed simulation model of police patrol operations was developed (Kolesar and Walker 1975). However, the only policy it was used to test—cross-sector patrol car dispatching—was never seriously considered by the department.

During this renewal of the Police Project, the issue of the mismatch between the number of cars actually fielded and the demand for emergency police service was revisited. Using a combination of optimization and queueing theory, the researchers generated a range of staffing options that were much more flexible than the dormant fourth platoon concept (Kolesar et al. 1975b). However, the concepts were never seriously considered for adoption by NYPD senior management and were formally abandoned after a successful court challenge by the police union (Moore et al. 1975). But the extent of the staffing mismatch was documented as never before, and a fourth platoon program was reinstituted in a scaled-down version staffed by police officers on a voluntary basis.

The most successful of the institute's police deployment models was the Patrol Car Allocation Model, or PCAM (Chaiken and Dormont 1978a, b). This queuing-based optimization model, described in more detail in the next section, created an efficient method for determining the allocation of patrol cars and officers across the seventy-odd police commands (precincts) of the city and across the three tours of duty. Like the firehouse-siting model, it played a critical role in determining the best way to reduce resources during the financial crisis of the 1970s. And, as with the firehouse-siting model, it was largely developed and disseminated to other cities with support from HUD, and was widely distributed to, and used by, other cities.

Though it was never implemented as part of the Police Project, the hypercube model (Larson 2001) was also partially funded by the NYCRI. It was used later in a study of travel times for the NYPD (Larson and Rich 1987), as well as to support the deployment of ambulances and police cars in various cities including New York, Boston, and Orlando (Brandeau and Larson 1986, Sacks and Grief 1994).

MANAGEMENT SCIENCE 1969–1989: A BOUNTY OF APPLICATIONS TO EMERGENCY SYSTEMS

Management Science published some of the earliest and most practically influential papers in the area of emergency response systems, many of which were a direct or indirect product of the New York City-based work described earlier. Here, we focus on these as well as other papers that described or resulted in implementations elsewhere.

Perhaps the earliest of these is a paper by Savas (1969) on a simulation analysis of the ambulance system in a single hospital district in Brooklyn exploring the potential improvements from proposed changes in the number and location of ambulances. This marked the first time that New York City used simulation as an aid in decision making. Before Savas' study, ambulances were located at each district's hospital. To reduce response times, a proposal had been made to station ambulances at satellite garages located in the middle of the highest demand areas. The simulation study indicated that this would substantially improve response times, and as a result a satellite was placed in the test district on a pilot basis. But a new and more fundamental recommendation emerged as well. It became evident that ambulances should be stationed close to the demand and not tied to hospital locations. This observation—that the transportation service could be divorced from the treatment centers—implied that ambulances should be centrally dispatched and managed, that they should be dispersed throughout the hospital district, and that they should be relocated as demand patterns change. Largely as a result of this work, New York City changed its policy and began to locate ambulances at curb sites, a practice that continues to this day.

This pioneering use of simulation and the resulting practical policy implications were a major impetus to the use of simulation and other quantitative modeling in emergency vehicle location. Among these was another early and influential *Management Science* publication by Fitzsimmons (1973), which focused on identifying optimal ambulance locations. Using an M/G/[infinity] queuing model combined with simulation, he estimated the probabilities of particular ambulances being busy assuming a given set of possible locations. This methodology was coupled with a pattern search routine in a computerized ambulance deployment model named CALL (Computerized Ambulance Location Logic), which identified ambulance locations that minimized mean response time. CALL was used successfully to choose 14 out of 34 possible firehouses at which to station ambulances in central Los Angeles and resulted in significant improvements in response times. It was also used to plan an emergency ambulance system for Melbourne, Australia. Another application of simulation to locate ambulances was described in an early *Management Science* paper by Swoveland et al. (1973), who developed a simulation model of the ambulance system in Vancouver, Canada, to estimate mean response times and other performance statistics for various possible ambulance locations and dispatch policies. They then used this output in a combinatorial optimization model to identify near-optimal ambulance locations.

To identify emergency vehicle locations that minimize total mean response time, it is necessary to estimate the average travel time as a function of any particular set of available units. It had already been demonstrated (Larson 1972) that the average travel distance in a region is inversely proportional to the square root of the number of available units per unit area. So, by using a queueing model to first obtain the probability distribution of the number of busy units in a region with N units, the square root model could be used to estimate distance, and hence travel time, for each possible system state. However, in a pivotal *Management Science* paper, Kolesar and Blum (1973) showed that the average travel distance is also approximately inversely proportional to the square root of the average number of available units per unit area. Thus the expected travel time could be estimated simply without the need of a queueing model. As mentioned previously, this square root model was used extensively by the RAND Fire Project, particularly to identify which fire companies to close and where to relocate others to improve response times (Kolesar and Walker 1974), as well as in many subsequent papers on emergency response planning and management (see, e.g., Swersey 1982, Ignall et al. 1982, Green and Kolesar 1984b, Halpern 1979).

The Kolesar and Blum square root model was the foundation for another important *Management Science* paper on allocating fire companies. Rider (1976) used the model to enable managers to incorporate non-quantifiable criteria into decision making about fire company allocations. Rider's Parametric Allocation Model used a parameter in the objective function of an optimization routine to represent the trade-off between minimizing citywide average travel time and equalizing average travel times across regions, where travel time was calculated using the Kolesar and Blum formula. This provided a more powerful tool for fire department managers, who could now consider a range of allocations and use personal judgment to choose one to achieve a desired balance of efficiency and equity. The Parametric Allocation Model has been used in several cities including Jersey City, New Jersey and Tacoma, Washington (Walker et al. 1979, pp. 349–364, 581–588).

Ambulance and fire systems were not the only beneficiaries of work that was published in *Management Science* in the 1970s and 1980s. Some of the most influential research was in the area of police patrol. One of the most widely disseminated models in the area of emergency responsiveness is the Patrol Car Allocation Model (PCAM), which was described in two *Management Science* papers by Chaiken and Dormont (1978a, b). PCAM, which was part of the NYCRI work, was developed as a result of senior NYPD management's interest in developing a quantitative, independently justifiable method for allocating police personnel to precincts. The patrol force allocation method generally favored before the RAND work used a subjectively weighted average measure of various disparate factors considered important by police departments in determining staffing levels, including precinct sizes, crime rates, and numbers of arrests. However, Larson had showed that these "hazard model" formulae did not actually work the way police commanders thought; PCAM's structure was a direct outgrowth of his work (Larson 1972, [section]1.4 and Chapter 5). Although various queueing-based models had already been developed for patrol allocation in New York City, St. Louis, Los Angeles, and Rotterdam, each had limitations that precluded its general usefulness. PCAM, which was designed after a review of these earlier programs, used an M/M/c queueing model with priority classes and could operate in either descriptive or prescriptive mode. It provided a variety of output measures, including the average queue time by priority class, the average travel time, patrol car utilization, and preventive patrol frequency. Average travel time was calculated using the square root formula of Kolesar and Blum (1973) described above, while the preventive patrol frequency used a formula developed by Larson (1972). It allowed an adjustment for noncall for service work, including activities such as meals, auto repairs, and special assignments, which was found to account for as much as 60% of total patrol time in some cities. In prescriptive mode, PCAM allocated car-hours to shifts where a shift is a combination of a specific tour of duty on a specific day in a specific precinct. This allowed users to implement tours with differing lengths. It also allowed for "overlay" tours, beginning during one standard tour and ending during another. PCAM could either determine the minimum number of cars needed in each shift to meet user-specified performance constraints, or allocate a fixed number of car-hours among precincts for a given shift or among shifts to minimize a given objective function. These features, which allowed police managers to specify inputs and outputs in ways that were meaningful to them, is what made PCAM so valuable and widely adopted.

PCAM was originally validated using data from New York City and was used during the financial crisis of the 1970s to make difficult decisions about cutbacks on patrol resources. It was ultimately distributed to over 40 police departments in the United States, to cities in Canada and the Netherlands, and to the single police force which covers all of Israel. In most of these locales, PCAM was implemented after parts or all of the model were validated using local data, and its use led to operational changes (Chaiken 1978, Lawless 1987).

One significant shortcoming of PCAM was that it did not explicitly represent multiple-car dispatches. Every police department receives some calls that require the services of more than one patrol car. In New York City, for example, over 30% of calls result in a multiple-car response. When the size of the patrol force relative to the call rate is large, a simple upward adjustment to the call arrival rate by the multiple-car dispatch ratio may result in fairly accurate predictions of delays. However, after the size of the New York City patrol force was reduced in the late 1970s, the NYPD found that despite such heuristic adjustments, PCAM was significantly underestimating actual delays (Green and Kolesar 1984a, 1989). This led them to contact Peter Kolesar to commission a revision of the model. Kolesar, in turn, enlisted his Columbia colleague, Linda Green, who had recently developed a queueing model in which the number of servers needed by a customer was random (Green 1980), and this resulted in Green's development of a multiple-car dispatch (MCD) queueing model of police patrol published in *Management Science* (Green 1984). The MCD model is a multiserver, multipriority Markovian queueing model in which the user specifies a probability distribution of the number of servers needed by each call for service type. In an extension of the basic model, both a minimum and maximum number of servers may be specified and the actual number used is dependent on server availability. In the MCD model, service to a job does not begin until the minimum number of required servers is available. Once service has begun, service times of cars are identically and independently distributed. Various performance measures are computed, including the probability of delay and mean delay by priority class and the average number of available servers. The MCD model was validated in New York City and incorporated in a revised version of PCAM (Green and Kolesar 1989, Chaiken et al. 1985) that was distributed through RAND to 46 police departments. It was also used in the evaluation of the proposed mergers of the police and fire departments in several cities (Chelst 1990) including Grosse Point Park, Michigan (Chelst 1988), where the analysis demonstrated that a merger could bring improvements in response times, patrol coverage, and operating expenses, and convinced voters to support it in a referendum.

The MCD model also played a central role in what would become a politically controversial study commissioned by the New York City mayor's office in 1981 to determine whether the NYPD should switch from two officers per patrol car to one. This study is described in another *Management Science* article (Green and Kolesar 1984b). The city was pursuing a gain-sharing program in negotiations with the police officers' union and wanted to determine how many more one-officer cars should be fielded to achieve the same average dispatch delay as with the current two-officer system. The Green and Kolesar study, employing the MCD model, showed that though a one-officer patrol system could achieve a significant reduction in police officers, about 40% more patrol cars would need to be fielded. This increase of cars in the street and "on-the-air" raised concerns on the researchers' part about the capability of the existing 911 management and communications system to coordinate the back-up car dispatch needed to assure patrol officer safety. No one, either in the mayor's office or in the NYPD, ever challenged the accuracy of the researchers' findings or conclusions. Indeed, senior NYPD commanders concurred with these concerns, and also with Green and Kolesar's suggestion that a carefully monitored experimental one-officer program be conducted in a limited number of precincts. The mayor's office, however, eager to demonstrate, or at least claim, productivity gains before an upcoming election, decided to pursue the program with neither further study nor a program to address the potential communications bottlenecks. When Green and Kolesar refused to support the city's intention to implement a broad one-officer program, the mayor's office withheld payment on part of their completed work and threatened a lawsuit to obtain the then unpublished MCD model. The mayor's office intended to provide the model to another OR/MS analyst who, it hoped, would support its position before the City Council. However, negotiations broke down after the police union's leaders, aware of the concerns raised in the Green and Kolesar analysis, insisted that the city guarantee that the number of cars fielded be adequate to assure rapid back-up, and the city refused. Over the next several years, the results of the Green and Kolesar study were used to justify the city's further exploration of one-officer patrol, which was ultimately implemented on a limited basis. (Green and Kolesar, however, though independently funded to continue their research on patrol deployment, were blacklisted from working for the city until the next administration came into office.)

In another influential *Management Science* paper, Chelst (1981) compared one- vs. two-officer patrol systems by estimating the differences in travel times for both first- and second-arriving units using an approach similar to Kolesar and Blum (1973). Chelst considered two different models of dispatch operations: a conventional "beat" system in which cars are assigned to a particular geographic region and, when available, respond to all calls originating in that region; and a system in which an automated vehicle monitoring system allows for cross beat dispatch of the unit closest to the incident. An important contribution of this paper was a clarification of workload conditions under which two one-officer cars could arrive at the scene faster than one two-officer car. In early 2003, the city of Buffalo, New York, facing bankruptcy, was considering a switch from a two- to one-officer patrol system with a 20% reduction in officers. Because of his *Management Science* paper, Chelst was asked to assess the impact of this proposed change and develop a patrol deployment plan. The subsequent study and testimony before the City Council led to a negotiated agreement with the police union to switch to a one-officer system in the summer of 2003 that resulted in a dramatic improvement in patrol response times (Warner 2003).

WHAT'S HAPPENED IN THE LAST 15 YEARS?

In total, between 1969 and 1989, over two dozen articles focusing on emergency response systems appeared in *Management Science*, many of which described new models that influenced actual operating policies and practices. Since that time, we were able to find only two articles in the journal on emergency systems (Rajan and Mannur 1990, Athanas-Sopoulos 1998), neither of which appears to have resulted in an actual application. This is a consistent with a general lack of papers in this area across all of the management science/ operations research journals starting in the 1990s. Why did this happen? Does this dearth of publication activity imply that there was a sharp decline in interest in, or need for, models to aid decision making in ambulance, fire, and police systems? And what, if anything, does this imply for the usefulness and use of the numerous models that were developed and implemented in the 1970s and 1980s?

There are several possible explanations for this decline in emergency response system publications. To some extent, the models developed in earlier decades had already addressed the most basic and important problems faced by the managers of emergency systems. In effect, much of the cream had been skimmed. Many of these models were widely known and disseminated through the efforts of RAND and the publication of two major books describing them: Urban Police Patrol (Larson 1972) and the Fire Department Deployment Analysis (Walker et al. 1979). Some of the models have been modified over the years by consulting organizations and incorporated into proprietary software packages, precluding open literature publication of these modifications. In addition, although there are gaps and flaws in the original models that could be addressed with more sophisticated approaches, increased complexity could be resisted by the managers and planners who use such models. Typical public sector technology transfer and implementation challenges are described in two studies published in *Management Science* (Chaiken 1978, Lawless 1987).

Another possible explanation is a diminished need for decision-support models in emergency response planning and management. As described previously, in the late 1960s to the mid-1970s large U.S. cities were confronting problems of increasing crime, drug abuse, and social and racial unrest. An economic downturn led to more arson-for-profit as distressed business owners torched their own premises to collect insurance money; "burn, baby, burn!" was a popular chant that reflected the climate of social protest. During this period, demand for emergency services grew and economic pressures constrained the available resources, making it imperative that emergency systems utilize their scarce resources as efficiently and effectively as possible. In contrast, the 1990s were a time of economic prosperity, low unemployment, and decreasing crime and turmoil. Staffing levels in police and fire departments were increased, and hence the need for "optimal" resource allocation became far less pressing.

The previous discussion highlights what we feel is a distinctive feature of research in emergency response systems: It is very difficult, if not impossible, to do without the sponsorship of a client organization. Unlike research in, for example, inventory management or queueing theory, which is often conceived of, and carried out by, individual academics scattered across the university landscape, meaningful models of emergency systems cannot be developed without intimate knowledge of the organization, its operations, and its objectives. When the need for such models is low and there is little political impulse to identify critical social problems, provide and focus funding, encourage cooperative partnerships, and guide implementation, scholars will find it very difficult to identify and/or implement a fruitful stream of research in the area on their own. One example is our work on staffing service systems that face time-varying customer demands (Green et al. 2001), which was originally motivated by our finding that the NYPD's use of the standard Erlang-based approach resulted in understaffing (Green and Kolesar 1989). This research led to the development of a simple heuristic that corrects the understaffing problem, but it was never implemented in the NYPD.

Moreover, it seems that an element in the success of the NYCRI effort was its large scale, temporal continuity, and unique mixture of consulting and research (Hayes 1972). A stable core team of about half a dozen Ph.D.-level OR/MS researchers stuck with a set of problems from conceptualization to implementation over a six-year period. Moreover, the analysts were amply supported by a staff of computer systems people, data analysts, and a management team that ran interference for them with the political establishment.

To gain more insight into the current need and use of management science models in emergency systems, we examined whether and how the models that were developed by the NYCRI are currently used in the NYPD and FDNY. We interviewed managers in the planning organizations of both departments to determine which models are still in use, how they are being used, and the extent to which senior managers see the models as useful for the problems their organizations are currently facing.

Our discussion with a group from the NYPD's Office of Management Analysis and Planning (OMAP) confirmed that the department still uses the revised version of PCAM that incorporates the MCD model (see the discussion in the previous section), but has changed the way in which it is used. First, and somewhat ironically, although the MCD model resulted from an explicit request by the NYPD to correct PCAM's inability to adequately account for the high level of multiple-car dispatches in New York City, OMAP does not implement this feature. This is despite the fact that the current fraction of 911 calls with multiple-car response is between 30% and 40%. Second, while the PCAM model was run in the 1980s on a monthly basis to adjust patrol-car allocations and staffing for seasonal changes in 911 demand patterns, its current use is mostly limited to providing an objective first step for "equitably" allocating the annual graduating class of police recruits among the city's 71 precincts according to several performance and workload measures.

This change in attitude and use of PCAM seems partly to be due to changes in NYPD management style, resources, and personnel. With the advent of the NYPD's COMPSTAT anticrime management system, which uses detailed, retrospective crime statistics to hold precinct commanders directly accountable for performance, dispatch delays are viewed as the result of individual precinct commanders' decisions on how to allocate their officers across competing assignments: responding to 911 calls, investigative work, addressing quality-of-life crimes, and special anticrime assignments; as well as how well they manage these officers. Moreover, there is now a relatively large patrol force available to deal with the stream of 911 calls, particularly those involving crimes in progress. The implicit assumption of the NYPD senior management seems to be that each precinct has enough resources to keep dispatch delays within desired standards and it is up to the precinct commander to determine how to do it (without the help of a PCAM model). This is in contrast to the late 1970s and early 1980s when, because of financial pressures, the size of the patrol force was repeatedly reduced while crime rates were very high. Finally, none of the current OMAP personnel has an OR/MS background, and their level of understanding of the model and its capabilities is generally limited. Of course, now it would be relatively simple to provide each precinct with its own laptop computer-based PCAM model, particularly because OMAP will soon be providing the precincts with the data needed to run it. Several precinct commanders, after learning of PCAM's capabilities during a Columbia-based educational program for senior officers of the NYPD, have expressed a strong interest in having this tool.

Meanwhile, the director of the NYPD's OMAP told us that PCAM was still seen as a valuable tool and that he would like an update of the PCAM computer code to "improve efficiency" and to take advantage of the kind of advanced mapping capabilities that are at the heart of COMPSTAT to improve patrol allocation and perhaps dispatch decisions. He also expressed a desire for a study on the effect of changing the current, sometimes "irrational," precinct boundaries, which can separate two sides of the same street into two different precincts. Another study on his wish list would look at the potential improvements that may be derived by changing the current tour design, which still segments the day into three nonoverlapping time periods and uses a suboptimal "fourth platoon" as described above, even though a RAND study (Kolesar et al. 1975) showed this to be grossly suboptimal 25 years ago.

We found a somewhat similar situation at the FDNY Division of Management Analysis & Planning. A dog-eared copy of the RAND Fire Project book was on the shelf at the FDNY's Management Analysis & Planning Division and an updated version of the firehouse-siting model was still being used. In fact, the model played an important role in supporting Mayor Bloomberg's recent and controversial decision to close six firehouses in the face of an almost $4 billion budget gap. This decision, like virtually all decisions to close firehouses, met with strong opposition from the affected communities and resulted in sustained demonstrations and hearings before the City Council (Colapinto 2003, McIntire 2003), where members questioned the model's validity. But in testimony before the City Council, the fire commissioner claimed that three months of postchange actual data confirmed the siting model's predictions that fire protection would not materially deteriorate. However, as with PCAM, our discussion revealed that none of the people running the siting model has an OR/MS background and, consequently, the way the model was used seemed suboptimal; the key response time measures were being calculated without weighting by incidence frequency. Somehow, over the years, the siting model's original capability to compute weighted average response times had been lost and no one understood the old computer code well enough to reinstitute this feature. Instead, the FDNY's analysts did ad hoc adjustments to the model's outputs to approximate the desired measures.

We also learned that the RAND-developed dynamic fire company relocation model was still in use, though it was now consulted less frequently than when first implemented during the years of high alarm rates in the late 1970s. But the algorithm played an important role when the World Trade Center disaster on September 11, 2001, emptied most of Manhattan and much of Brooklyn of fire protection. More than 200 fire companies responded to the Twin Towers location, approximately half the entire city's complement, and the relocation algorithm was used to help rebalance the remaining resources in the city by relocating several dozen companies. The combination of the decision support provide by the algorithm, the sound judgment of the chiefs in charge, and the heroic efforts of the firefighters maintained fire protection at adequate levels throughout the rest of the city despite 9/11 being an otherwise average alarm rate day. A thorough picture of the FDNY's response to this disaster, coupled with numerous recommendations for improvements in communications and logistical planning for possible future disasters, is contained in the report by McKinsey & Company (McKinsey & Company 2002).

The specter of future terrorist events has prompted FDNY interest in augmenting the capabilities of the dynamic relocation algorithm to include real-time evaluations of alternative relocations suggested by chiefs or dispatchers in terms of expected response times in the affected area. The 9/11 experience has also prompted an application by the FDNY to secure funding from the Department of Homeland Security to develop a siting model for ambulances, which the department has been managing since they were given responsibility for Emergency Medical Systems several years ago.

Several observations emerged from our conversations with the two agencies. First, there is a continued appreciation and understanding of the need for computer models to support operational decision making. A dramatic example of this is COMPSTAT, the much recognized and imitated NYPD management innovation that has been credited as a major factor in the city's more than 60% reduction in crime over the last decade (but which currently incorporates no statistical or OR/MS models or analysis). Second, the development of information and communications technology makes possible approaches to deployment that were technologically or economically infeasible when emergency service modeling was at its height in the 1970s. Third, there are many challenges to the continued effective use of such a model after it is developed. These include changes in the management environment of the host agency, the need to maintain and update software and hardware, and personnel changes that result in the model being used by people who do not adequately understand how or why the model does what it does. Finally, and perhaps most importantly, the managers at both the NYPD and FDNY expressed the need and desire for new management science models to help with current issues of importance.

SO WHAT DOES THE FUTURE HOLD?

The advent of 9/11 and broad threats of domestic terrorism has given rise to an entirely different perspective on emergency responsiveness. Managers of police, fire, and ambulance systems, as well as mayors and governors, must now think about how to prepare and plan for catastrophic events that were previously unthinkable. As indicated by our conversation with the FDNY, 9/11 has created a new imperative for management science models and analyses to help design emergency systems and plans for responding to and minimizing the impact of terrorist attacks or other potentially large-scale emergencies. The reaction to the 9/11 attacks has also created a source of funding for research through the U.S. Department of Homeland Security. Some of this funding is allocated directly to municipalities and states through the Office of Domestic Preparedness. Other funding, through the Science and Technology division, is targeted for creating Centers of Excellence in universities to conduct multidisciplinary research to "enhance our ability to anticipate, prevent, respond to, and recover from terrorist attacks" (see Department of Homeland Security 2003). The first such center was created in November 2003 at the University of Southern California. Though this center is primarily focused on risk analysis related to the economic consequences of terrorist threats and events, it will contain a component addressing the development of models for emergency responsiveness. Future centers may include one that is focused exclusively on the latter. One might hope this could create an institution akin to the NYCRI with the potential to bring together a team of talented operations researchers focused on important problems of emergency responsiveness that has sufficient funding to sustain modeling and analysis over a period of years.

However, experience and history tell us that the potential for implementation and impact of new models and analysis will rest on several other factors as well. First, there is a need for well-defined client organizations that can act as full-fledged partners in the development of models to ensure their usefulness and actual implementation. Institutional and/or political leadership, as existed, for example, in the FDNY during the NYCRI era, is necessary to champion what may be controversial suggestions about new policies and practices. For example, the very fine work of Kaplan et al. (2002), which demonstrated the superiority of a mass vaccination program to minimize deaths resulting from a smallpox attack, met with significant political resistance from some public health officials and institutions, and implementation has been delayed. Also, as we learned from NYPD's experience with PCAM, the sustainability of any new operational support system depends heavily on the degree to which there exists in the client agency an influential and technically competent planning organization with the ability to effectively use, maintain, and upgrade models over the years.

An additional obstacle to implementation of a new generation of emergency service decision support models dealing with high-impact emergencies is that resulting policies and plans will almost certainly involve coordination of various agencies and geographic regions. This greatly complicates both the politics and logistics of implementation. Another distinction is that unlike "routine" emergencies, which, by definition, occur regularly and for which there is ample data, there is no practical way to validate models of 9/11-type of events. This presents additional hurdles in establishing the credibility of models and in identifying unanticipated consequences and the nonobvious factors that need to be addressed.

Despite these challenges, the history of success in using modeling and analysis in emergency planning and responsiveness, as described in many *Management Science* articles as well as elsewhere, demonstrates that our field can and should play an important role in minimizing the impact of both routine and catastrophic emergencies in the future. We may now be facing an unprecedented opportunity to use our unique skills and experience to influence the collective welfare, and in doing so, recapture some of the energy and excitement that emanated from the origins of our field during World War II.

Linda V. Green, Peter J. Kolesar, Graduate School of Business, Columbia University, New York, New York 1002

ACKNOWLEDGMENTS

The authors wish to thank Andrea Allocca of the FDNY and Chief John Gerrish of the NYPD for meeting with us on current operations in their departments. Ed Blum, Jan Chaiken, Ken Chelst, Ed Kaplan, Dick Larson, Randy Hall, Art Swersey, Warren Walker, and Larry Wein offered valuable input and comments.
Key words: applications; emergency services; fire; police; public sector; urban

NOTES

1.   For one of the few examples of RAND's military work that is unclassified, see Wohlstetter et al. (1954).

2.   More details can be found in Drake et al. (1972), particularly in Chapters 1, 2, 7, and 9; in Greenberger et al. (1976), particularly in Chapters 7, 8, and 9; and in Walker et al. (1979, pp. 629–639).

3. Searching on the key words "fire" and "police" will lead to most of the publications related to emergency service deployment.

4. A contemporaneous viewpoint on this work by the then fire commissioner can be found in O'Hagan (1973).

REFERENCES

Archibald, R. W., R. B. Hoffman. 1969. Introducing technological change in a bureaucratic structure. New York City-RAND Institute, P-4025, New York.

Athanassopoulos, A. D. 1998. Decision support for target-based resource allocation of public services in multiunit and multilevel systems. *Management Sci.* 44(2) 173–187.

Blum, E. H. 1972. The New York City fire project. A. Drake, R. Keeney, P. Morse, eds. *Analysis of Public Systems*, Ch. 7. MIT Press, Cambridge, MA.

Blumstein, A. 2002. Crime modeling. *Oper. Res.* 50(1) 16–24.

Brandeau, M., R. C. Larson. 1986. Extending and applying the hypercube queueing model to deploy ambulances in Boston. A. Swersey, E. Ignall, eds. *Delivery of Urban Services*, Invited Chapter. North-Holland, New York.

Carter, G., E. Ignall. 1970. A simulation model of fire department operations. IEEE Trans. *Systems Sci. Cybernetics* SCC-6(4) 282–293.

Carter, G., E. Ignall. 1975. Virtual measures: A variance reduction technique for simulation. *Management Sci.* 21(6) 607–616.

Carter, G., J. Rolph. 1973. New York City fire alarm prediction models: I. Box reported serious fires. Report R-1214-NYC, The RAND Corporation, Santa Monica, CA.

Carter, G., J. Rolph. 1974. Empirical Bayes methods applied to estimating fire alarm probabilities. *J. Amer. Statist. Assoc.* 69(348) 880–885.

Carter, G., J. Chaiken, E. Ignall. 1972. Response areas for two emergency units. *Oper. Res.* 20(3) 571–594.

Chaiken, J. M. 1978. Transfer of emergency service deployment models to operating agencies. *Management Sci.* 24(7) 719–731.

Chaiken, J. M., P. Dormont. 1978a. A patrol car allocation model: Background. *Management Sci.* 24(12) 1280–1290.

Chaiken, J. M., P. Dormont. 1978b. A patrol car allocation model: Capabilities and algorithms, *Management Sci.* 24(12) 1291–1300.

Chaiken, J. M., E. Ignall. 1972. An extension of Erlang's formulas which distinguishes individual servers. *J. Appl. Probab.* 9(1) 192–197.

Chaiken, J., W. Walker, P. Dormont. 1985. Patrol car allocation model: Executive summary. Report R-3087/3-NIJ, The RAND Corporation, Santa Monica, CA.

Chaiken, J., E. Ignall, P. Kolesar, W. Walker. 1980. Response to the communication on RAND-HUD fire models. *Management Sci.* 26(4) 422–432.

Chelst, K. 1981. Deployment of one- vs. two-officer patrol units: A comparison of travel times. *Management Sci.* 27(12) 213–230.

Chelst, K. 1988. A public safety merger in Grosse Pointe Park, Michigan—A short and sweet study. *Interfaces* 18(4) 1–11.

Chelst, K. 1990. Queueing models for police-fire merger analysis. Queueing Systems 7 101–124.

Colapinto, J. 2003. The untouchables. *New York Times Magazine* (October 5) 54–59.

Daley, R. 1973. *Target Blue*. Delacourt Press, New York.

Department of Homeland Security. 2003. http://www.dhs.gov.

Dickson, P. 1971. *Think Tanks*. Ballantine Books, New York, 249.

Dormont, P., J. Hausner, W. Walker. 1975. Firehouse site evaluation model: Description and users manual. Report R-1618-2-HUD, The RAND Corporation, Santa Monica, CA.

Drake, A., R. Keeney, P. Morse, eds. 1972. *Analysis of Public Systems*. MIT Press, Cambridge, MA.

Fitzsimmons, J. A. 1973. A methodology for emergency ambulance deployment. *Management Sci.* 19(6) 627–636.

Green, L. 1980. A queueing system in which customers require a random number of servers. *Oper. Res.* 28 1335–1346.

Green, L. 1984. A multiple dispatch queueing model of police patrol operations. *Management Sci.* 30(6) 653–664.

Green, L., P. Kolesar. 1984a. A comparison of the multiple dispatch and M/M/c priority queueing models of police patrol. *Management Sci.* 30(6) 665–670.

Green, L., P. Kolesar. 1984b. The feasibility of one-officer patrol in New York City. *Management Sci.* 30(8) 964–981.

Green, L., P. Kolesar. 1989. Testing the validity of a queueing model of police patrol. *Management Sci.* 35(2) 127–148.

Green, L., P. Kolesar, J. Soares. 2001. Improving the SIPP approach for staffing service systems that have cyclic demands. *Oper. Res.* 49(4) 549–564.

Greenberger, M., M. A. Crenson, B. L. Crissey. 1976. *Models in the Policy Process*. The Russell Sage Foundation, Basic Books, New York.

Halpern, J. 1979. Fire loss reduction: Fire detectors vs. fire stations. *Management Sci.* 25(11) 1082–1092.

Hayes, F. 1972. From inside the system. A. Drake, R. Keeney, P. Morse, eds. *Analysis of Public Systems,* Ch. 1. MIT Press, Cambridge, MA.

Henry, V. 2002. *The Compstat Paradigm: Management Accountability in Policing, Business and the Public Sector*. Looseleaf Law Publications, New York.

Hitch, C. 1960. *The Economics of Defense in a Nuclear Age*. Harvard University Press, Cambridge, MA.

Hogg, J. 1968. The siting of fire stations. *Oper. Res.* Quart. 19 275–287.

Hoos, I. 1972. *Systems Analysis in Public Policy: A Critique*. University of California Press, Berkeley, CA.

Ignall, E., G. Carter, K. Rider. 1982. An algorithm for the initial dispatch of fire companies. *Management Sci.* 28(4) 366–378.

Ignall, E., P. Kolesar, A. Swersey, W. Walker, E. Blum, G. Carter, H. Bishop. 1975. Improving the deployment of New York City's fire companies. *Interfaces* 5(2) 48–61.

Kaplan, E. H., D. L. Craft, L. M. Wein. 2002. Emergency response to a smallpox attack. *Proc. National Acad. Sci.* 99 10935–10940.

Knapp, W. 1972. Summary and principal recommendations of the commission to investigate allegations of police corruption. The Fund for the City of New York, New York.

Kolesar, P., E. H. Blum. 1973. Square root laws for fire engine response distances. *Management Sci.* 19(12) 1368–1378.

Kolesar, P., K. L. Rider. 1981. The fire department. C. Bresher, R. D. Horton, eds. *Setting Municipal Priorities* 1982, Ch. 9. Russell Sage Foundation, Basic Books, New York.

Kolesar, P., A. Swersey. 1986. The deployment of urban emergency units: A survey. A. Swersey, E. Ignall, eds. *Delivery of Urban Services. Studies in the Management Sciences,* Vol. 22. North-Holland, New York, 87–120.

Kolesar, P., W. E. Walker. 1974. An algorithm for the dynamic relocation of fire companies. *Oper. Res.* 22(2) 249–274.

Kolesar, P., W. E. Walker. 1975. A simulation model of police patrol operations. Report R-1625-NYC/HUD, The RAND Corporation, Santa Monica, CA.

Kolesar, P., W. E. Walker, J. Hausner. 1975a. Determining the relation between fire engine travel times and travel distances in New York City companies. *Oper. Res.* 23(4) 614–627.

Kolesar, P., K. Rider, T. Crabill, W. Walker. 1975b. A queueing linear programming approach to scheduling police cars. Oper. Res. 23 1045–1062.

Koopman, B. O. 1956a. The theory of search part I: Kinematic bases. *Oper. Res.* 4 324–346.

Koopman, B. O. 1956b. The theory of search part II: Target detection. Oper. Res. 4 503–531.

Koopman, B. O. 1957. The theory of search part III: The optimum distribution of searching effect. *Oper. Res.* 5 613–626.

Larson, R. C. 1972. *Urban Police Patrol Analysis.* MIT Press, Cambridge, MA.

Larson, R. C. 2001. Hypercube queueing model. S. I. Gass, C. M. Harris, eds. *Encyclopedia of Operations Research and Management Science.* Centennial Edition, Kluwer, Boston, MA, 373–377.

Larson, R. C. 2002. Public sector operations research: A personal journey. *Oper. Res.* 50(1) 135–145.

Larson, R. C., T. Rich. 1987. Travel time analysis of New York City police patrol cars. *Interfaces* 17(2) 15–20.

Lawless, M. W. 1987. Institutionalization of management science innovation in police department. *Management Sci.* 33(2) 244–252.

MacDonald, H. 2001. Using Compstat against terror: NYPD crime busting system will work against Bin Laden. *New York Daily News* (November 4).

Maltz, M. D. 1994. Operations research in studying crime and justice: Its history and accomplishments. S. M. Pollock, M. H. Rothkopf, A. Barnett, eds. *Handbooks in Operations Research and Management Science,* Vol. 6. North-Holland, Amsterdam, The Netherlands, 201–253.

McIntire, M. 2003. City says closings slow fire response in six areas. *New York Times* (October 2) B4.

McKinsey & Company. 2002. Increasing FDNY's preparedness. Report to the City of New York, New York, http://www.nyc.gov/html/fdny/html/mck_report/toc.html.

Moore, M., G. Allison, T. Bates, J. Downing. 1975. The fourth platoon. Case C14-75-013, Kennedy School of Government, Harvard University, Cambridge, MA.

Murphy, P. V. 1977. *Commissioner: A View from the Top of American Law Enforcement.* Simon & Shuster, New York.

O'Hagan, J. 1973. Improving the deployment of fire fighting resources. *Fire J.* 67(4) 42–46.

Rajan, B., N. R. Mannur. 1990. Covering-location models for emergency situations that require multiple response units. *Management Sci.* 36(1) 16–23.

RAND Corporation. 1973. RAND 25th Anniversary Volume. The RAND Corporation, Santa Monica, CA.

Ranzel, E. 1970. Garelick calls RAND study of city's police a failure. *New York Times* (October 7).

Rider, K. L. 1976. A parametric model for the allocation of fire companies in New York City. *Management Sci.* 23(2) 146–158.

Sacks, S., S. Grief. 1994. Orlando magic. *OR/MS Today* 21(1) 30–32.

Savas, E. S. 1969. Simulation and cost-effectiveness analysis of New York's emergency ambulance service. *Management Sci.* 15(12) B608-B627.

Savas, E. S. 1973. The political properties of crystalline H2O: Planning for snow emergencies in New York. *Management Sci.* 20 137–145.

Savas, E. S. 1978. On equity in providing public services. *Management Sci.* 24(8) 800–808.

Smith, D. 1969. *Report from Engine Company 82.* Warner Books, New York.

Swersey, A. J. 1982. A Markovian decision model for deciding how many fire companies to dispatch. *Management Sci.* 28(4) 352–365.

Swersey, A. J. 1994. The deployment of police, fire and emergency medical units. S. M. Pollock, M. Rothkopf, A. Barnett, eds. *Handbooks in Operations Research and Management Science,* Vol. 6. North-Holland, New York, 151–190.

Swoveland, C., D. Uyeno, I. Vertinsky, R. Vickson. 1973. Ambulance locations: A probabilistic enumeration approach. *Management Sci.* 29 686–698.

Szanton, P. 1972. Analysis and urban government. A. Drake, R. Kenney, P. Morse, eds. *Analysis of Public Systems,* Ch. 2. MIT Press, Chambridge, MA.

Valinsky, D. 1955. A determination of the optimum location of fire-fighting units in New York City. *Oper. Res.* 4(3) 494–512.

Walker, W. 1975. Firehouse site evaluation model: Executive summary. Report R-1618-1-HUD, The RAND Corporation, Santa Monica, CA.

Walker, W., J. Chaiken, E. Ignall, eds. 1979. Fire Department Deployment Analysis: A Public Policy Analysis Case Study: The RAND Fire Project. North-Holland, New York.

Wallace, D., R. Wallace. 1999. *A Plague on Your House: How New York Burned Down and National Public Health Crumbled.* Verso Press, New York.

Wallace, R., D. Wallace. 1980. RAND—HUD fire models. *Management Sci.* 26(4) 418–422.

Warner, G. 2003. One-officer patrol cars improve response time. *Buffalo News* (August 10).

Wohlstetter, A. J., F. S. Hoffman, R. J. Lutz, H. S. Rowen. 1954. Selection and use of strategic air bases. Report R-266, The RAND Corporation, Santa Monica, CA.

Worth, R. 2003. Times change, officials say, and so fire houses are closing. *New York Times* (April 11) D1.

InfoMarks: Make Your Mark

What Is an InfoMark?

It is a single-click return ticket to any page, any result or any search from InfoTrac College Edition.

An InfoMark is a stable URL, linked to InfoTrac College Edition articles that you have selected. InfoMarks can be used like any other URL, but they're better because they're stable—they don't change. Using an InfoMark is like performing the search again whenever you follow the link, whether the result is a single article or a list of articles.

How Do InfoMarks Work?

If you can "copy and paste," you can use InfoMarks.

When you see the InfoMark icon on a result page, its URL can be copied and pasted into your electronic document—web page, word processing document, or email. Once InfoMarks are incorporated into a document, the results are persistent (the URLs will not change) and are dynamic.

Even though the saved search is used at different times by different users, an InfoMark always functions like a brand new search. Each time a saved search is executed, it accesses the latest updated information. That means subsequent InfoMark searches might yield additional or more up-to-date information than the original search with less time and effort.

Capabilities

InfoMarks are the perfect technology tool for creating:

- Virtual online readers
- Current awareness topic sites—links to periodical or newspaper sources
- Online/distance learning courses
- Bibliographies, reference lists
- Electronic journals and periodical directories
- Student assignments
- Hot topics

Advantages

- Select from over 15 million articles from more than 5,000 journals and periodicals
- Update article and search lists easily
- Articles are always full-text and include bibliographic information
- All articles can be viewed online, printed, or emailed
- Saves professors and students time
- Anyone with access to InfoTrac College Edition can use it
- No other online library database offers this functionality
- FREE!

How to Use InfoMarks

There are three ways to utilize InfoMarks—in HTML documents, Word documents, and Email

HTML Document

1. Open a new document in your HTML editor (Netscape Composer or FrontPage Express).
2. Open a new browser window and conduct your search in InfoTrac College Edition.
3. Highlight the URL of the results page or article that you would like to InfoMark.
4. Right-click the URL and click Copy. Now, switch back to your HTML document.
5. In your document, type in text that describes the InfoMarked item.
6. Highlight the text and click on Insert, then on Link in the upper bar menu.
7. Click in the link box, then press the "Ctrl" and "V" keys simultaneously and click OK. This will paste the URL in the box.
8. Save your document.

Word Document

1. Open a new Word document.
2. Open a new browser window and conduct your search in InfoTrac College Edition.
3. Check items you want to add to your Marked List.
4. Click on Mark List on the right menu bar.
5. Highlight the URL, right-click on it, and click Copy. Now, switch back to your Word document.
6. In your document, type in text that describes the InfoMarked item.
7. Highlight the text. Go to the upper bar menu and click on Insert, then on Hyperlink.

8. Click in the hyperlink box, then press the "Ctrl" and "V" keys simultaneously and click OK. This will paste the URL in the box.
9. Save your document.

Email

1. Open a new email window.
2. Open a new browser window and conduct your search in InfoTrac College Edition.
3. Highlight the URL of the results page or article that you would like to InfoMark.
4. Right-click the URL and click Copy. Now, switch back to your email window.
5. In the email window, press the "Ctrl" and "V" keys simultaneously. This will paste the URL into your email.
6. Send the email to the recipient. By clicking on the URL, he or she will be able to view the InfoMark.